I0007779

JANE FLORINS

Real UX: Practical Guide

Copyright © 2023 by Jane Florins

All rights reserved. No part of this publication may be reproduced, stored or transmitted in any form or by any means, electronic, mechanical, photocopying, recording, scanning, or otherwise without written permission from the publisher. It is illegal to copy this book, post it to a website, or distribute it by any other means without permission.

Jane Florins has no responsibility for the persistence or accuracy of URLs for external or third-party Internet Websites referred to in this publication and does not guarantee that any content on such Websites is, or will remain, accurate or appropriate.

Designations used by companies to distinguish their products are often claimed as trademarks. All brand names and product names used in this book and on its cover are trade names, service marks, trademarks and registered trademarks of their respective owners. The publishers and the book are not associated with any product or vendor mentioned in this book. None of the companies referenced within the book have endorsed the book.

First edition

Illustration by https://designs.ai/
Advisor: Michelle Lisak

This book was professionally typeset on Reedsy.
Find out more at reedsy.com

Contents

Intro

Welcome to the thrilling and ever-changing world of UX design! This book is the ultimate guide, specifically tailored for beginner UX designers with basic knowledge of UX design theory but limited practical experience.

Join us on a comprehensive journey through the classic UX process, comparing what's taught in schools to the reality of working in the field. As a budding UX designer, you may have encountered obstacles like balancing user needs with stakeholder demands or conducting user research in unfamiliar areas. Fear not, we're here to help!

We'll delve into the unique challenges of UX in different industries and company sizes and examine how UX teams are organized, providing you with a deeper understanding of the field.

Discover an abundance of tips, tricks, and insights to tackle the unique challenges of UX design. Learn how to handle conflicting opinions, tight deadlines, manage stakeholder expectations, and conduct effective user research like a pro. Additionally, we'll provide valuable advice on creating a stunning portfolio and landing your dream UX design job.

So, buckle up and get ready for an exhilarating ride in UX design. Grab your preferred design tool, a cup of strong coffee, and let's explore the exciting journey ahead together!

* * *

Chapter 1: The UX Reality Check

Welcome to the UX design process, where we take a simple concept like "making a user-friendly product" and turn it into a rigid, inflexible process that will leave you feeling like you're trying to navigate a maze blindfolded. Our process involves a series of steps, starting with user research and ideation, followed by wireframing, prototyping, and usability testing. These initial stages lay the foundation for the more intricate and demanding steps that come after, including visual design, development, and finally, launch.

> User experience is everything. It always has been, but it's under-valued and under-invested in. If you don't know user-centered design, study it. Hire people who know it. Obsess over it. Live and breathe it. Get your whole company on board.
>
> Evan Williams, Co-founder of Twitter

But fear not, dear reader, because our process ensures that the end product will not only be functional but also visually appealing and intuitive to use. It's like taking a stroll through a perfectly manicured garden, where every step is carefully planned out to ensure maximum enjoyment.

So strap on your hiking boots and get ready for a journey that will make you question every decision you've ever made. Just don't forget to bring a map, a compass, and a few snacks to keep you going. Because in the world of UX design, it's not about the destination, it's about the process. And boy, is it a process.

Foundations of UX: Understanding the Classic Process

The classic UX methodology has been the foundation of user-centered design for years, serving as a tried and true framework for creating intuitive and enjoyable products. With its well-defined stages and structured approach, the classic process has been a go-to framework for many UX designers. However, as the field of UX continues to evolve and adapt to real-world challenges, it's important to revisit and understand the classic methodology in the context of modern design practices. In this chapter, we will delve into the principles, methods, and techniques of the classic UX approach, examining its strengths, limitations, and how it compares to real-life UX workflows. So, let's take a closer look at the foundations of the classic UX methodology and explore how it has shaped the field of user experience design.

Step 1: User Research

User research is where we put on our detective hats and channel our inner Sherlock Holmes to uncover the needs, behaviors, and pain points of our users. We conduct interviews, surveys, and observe their behavior to create personas that represent our target audience. Personas are like our imaginary friends, except they keep us grounded and remind us to design with empathy.

Step 2: Ideation

Ideation is where we let our creativity run wild and gather a diverse group of people in a room to brainstorm ideas. It's like a fun game of improv where there are no wrong answers, just a plethora of ideas waiting to be explored. We use techniques like brainstorming, mind mapping, and sticky notes to capture all the crazy ideas that come up during this exciting phase of the design process.

Step 3: Wireframing

Wireframing is where we turn our brainstormed ideas into tangible concepts. We create low-fidelity sketches that represent the basic layout and functionality of the product, much like building the foundation of a house before adding all the fancy decorations. We then test and iterate on these wireframes until the concept starts to take shape, ensuring that the design meets the needs of the users and aligns with the overall vision of the product. It's like sculpting a rough clay model before refining it into a masterpiece!

Step 4: Prototyping

Prototyping is the stage where we bring our product to life. We create interactive mockups that simulate the appearance and functionality of the final product. It's similar to building a miniature model of a house to evaluate the design in real-world scenarios. We conduct thorough testing, refinement, and iteration until we have a prototype that effectively caters to the needs of our users.

Step 5: Usability Testing

Usability testing is where we invite our users for a playdate and observe them as they interact with our prototype. It's like having a focus group, but instead of selling them a product, we're learning from them. We keenly observe, ask questions, and take notes to gather valuable feedback on the user experience. This helps us identify any pain points or areas of improvement, so we can make our design even better. It's an invaluable opportunity to understand how real users engage with our product and make it more user-friendly and effective.

Step 6: Visual Design

During the visual design phase, we tap into our creativity to develop a unique visual language that represents the product's brand. We meticulously choose colors, typography, and imagery that are in harmony with the brand and generate high-fidelity mockups that illustrate the final product. This phase is similar to decorating a house with furniture and artwork to establish a warm and inviting ambiance. We analyze every aspect to create a visually striking and coherent design that connects with our intended audience. Visual design is the last step that perfects our product's appearance, making it aesthetically impressive and unforgettable.

Step 7: Development

Development is the stage where we bring our creation to life with code. We build the product's architecture and functionality, integrating it with third-party services. It's similar to constructing a robot from scratch, without a manual, and learning as we go. Just like a robot, our product starts taking shape as we meticulously code and test its features, ensuring they work seamlessly together. Development requires skill, creativity, and problem-solving to bring our design to life in a functional and interactive way.

Step 8: Launch

Launch is where we take our creation out into the world and share it with others. It's similar to sending your child off to college and hoping they'll make you proud. We monitor the performance of our product, gather user feedback, and make necessary updates and improvements. Just like parenting, the journey of a product is never truly over. We continue to iterate, refine, and adapt to the ever-evolving needs of our users and the market.

> **"The UX process is not just about making a product easy to use, but also making it enjoyable and memorable for users."**
>
> Don Norman, Director of the Design Lab at the University of California, San Diego

While the classic UX process can be time-consuming and costly, it's a reliable framework for delivering successful products, or at least that's what we tell ourselves. But let's be real, the classic UX process isn't always practical in the real world. Sometimes you need to make decisions quickly and can't afford to spend weeks on research and testing. That's where the real-world rough UX process comes in, like sprinting to catch the bus instead of leisurely walking to the station. It may not be as pretty or as thorough, but sometimes it's necessary to get the job done in a timely manner.

The Real World Rough UX Process - When Theory Meets Reality

Welcome to the wild, wild world of UX design in the real world, where timelines are nothing but a suggestion and resources are as rare as a unicorn. In this chapter, we'll hold your hand and guide you through the tough challenges of navigating the real-world UX process like a seasoned pro.

First up, we have **user research**. Forget those detailed research and persona creations you did in school. In the real world, deadlines, frequent changes, and budgets mean you have to work smarter, not harder. We'll show you how to gather insights quickly and efficiently using techniques like rapid surveys, secondary research, and expert interviews.

Next, we'll dive into the **ideation** phase. You may not have the luxury of endless brainstorming sessions, but don't worry - we've got your back. We'll share tips for being creative and flexible with limited time and resources, including techniques like design sprints, concept sketching, and leveraging pre-existing design systems.

Once you've got some rough ideas down, it's time to move on to **prototyping**. We'll discuss the different types of prototypes you might create in the real world, from low-fidelity paper prototypes to high-fidelity interactive prototypes. We'll also show you how to create prototypes quickly and efficiently, using tools like design systems, templates, and rapid prototyping software.

And finally, we come to **testing**. Sure, extensive user testing and valuable feedback would be ideal, but let's be real - you might need to rely on other methods like heuristic evaluation, expert review, or guerrilla testing. Don't fret, we'll show you how to conduct quick and effective tests that can help you make informed decisions.

Throughout the chapter, we'll explore the challenges of working with the real-world UX process, including tight deadlines, limited resources, and shifting project requirements. We'll share real-world examples and insights from experienced UX designers, so you can learn from their successes and failures. By the end of this chapter, you'll be well-equipped to handle any UX design challenge thrown your way. So, buckle up, and let's get started!

User Research - When Time and Resources Are Against You

Ah, user research. The backbone of any good UX design process. But what happens when you're working in the real world and you don't have the luxury of time and resources? Well, my friend, you'll have to get creative.

In school, you might have spent weeks conducting in-depth user interviews and creating detailed personas. But in the real world, you might only have a few days, or even hours, to gather insights. So, how do you do it? Here are some tips:

Rapid Surveys: Want to get a quick pulse on your user base? Create a rapid survey and blast it out on social media or through your company's email list. Keep it short and sweet, with no more than five questions. Make sure you're asking the right questions to get the answers you need.

Imagine you're working on a mobile app for a startup company and you need to gather insights about user preferences and behaviors within a tight timeline. You create a rapid survey with questions about their preferred features, usage patterns, and pain points. You share the survey on social media, send it through the company's email list, and even offer incentives for participation. Within a few days, you receive a significant number of responses that provide valuable insights for your design decisions, despite the time constraints.

Secondary Research: No time to conduct your own research? No problem. Dig through previous projects, academic research papers, and industry reports to gather insights on your user base. It's not as good as conducting your own research, but it's better than nothing.

Suppose you're tasked with redesigning a website for an e-commerce platform, and you have limited time for user research. Instead of conducting your own research, you dig through previous customer feedback, reviews, and analytics data to gather insights on user behavior, preferences, and pain points. You also review industry reports and competitor analysis to understand the market trends and user expectations. These secondary research findings provide valuable information that helps you make informed design decisions, even with limited time for primary research.

Expert Interviews: If you have access to subject matter experts, take advantage of it. Experts can provide valuable insights into your user base that you might not be able to gather through other means. Schedule a quick interview and pick their brain.

Let's say you're working on a healthcare app that requires a deep understanding of medical terminology and user needs. Despite limited time for user interviews, you schedule quick interviews with subject matter experts, such as doctors, nurses, and medical professionals, who can provide valuable insights on the target user base. Through these expert interviews, you gain valuable insights into user preferences, workflows, and pain points, which inform your design decisions and help create a user-centered experience.

But let's be honest, conducting user research in the real world can be fraught with challenges. Tight deadlines, limited budgets, a lack of resources, constantly changing requirements, and never-ending technical limitations are common obstacles that UX researchers often encounter. However, the key is to remain flexible, creative, and adaptable in order to work within these constraints. With a problem-solving mindset and a willingness to think outside the box, these challenges can be overcome, and valuable insights can still be gleaned from user research efforts. It may require innovative approaches, such as leveraging alternative research methods or finding creative solutions to technical limitations, but the end goal of creating user-friendly digital experiences is worth the effort.

At the end of the day, you might not have the most detailed personas, but you'll still have valuable insights that can inform your design decisions. Just remember to stay open-minded, stay agile, and keep pushing forward.

The Ideation Struggle - Creative Solutions for Limited Time and Resources

Welcome to the exciting world of ideation! In school, you may have had more time to brainstorm, sketch, and daydream about the perfect design. But in the real world, you have to work with tight deadlines and limited resources. So, how can you come up with brilliant ideas without sacrificing quality? Let's explore some practical advice and real-world examples:

Embrace Design Sprints: Design sprints are a structured process that can help your team generate ideas quickly and efficiently. Set a specific problem to solve, gather your team in a room (or virtually), and set a time limit. Use techniques like **rapid sketching**, **brainwriting**, and **collaborative activities** to generate as many ideas as possible. For example, a UX team at a digital agency used a design sprint to come up with ideas for improving the onboarding process of a mobile app. They set a one-hour time limit and used sticky notes to capture their ideas, resulting in a wealth of creative solutions.

Try Concept Sketching: Concept sketching is a rapid way to generate ideas without getting caught up in details. Grab a whiteboard, a notepad, or even a napkin, and start sketching out **rough concepts**. Don't worry about perfection, just focus on getting your ideas out quickly. For instance, a UX designer at a startup used concept sketching to explore different layout options for a website redesign. They quickly sketched out various wireframes on a whiteboard, allowing the team to visualize different design possibilities and iterate on them rapidly.

Leverage Pre-Existing Design Systems: Why reinvent the wheel when there are already plenty of amazing design frameworks and UI kits available? Use pre-existing **design systems** as a starting point to save time and resources. Customize and build upon them to fit your specific needs. Just remember to give credit to the original creators and follow any licensing requirements. For example, a UX team at a large e-commerce company used a popular design system to create a consistent user interface across multiple products. They customized the design system components to match their brand and product requirements, saving valuable time and effort.

Be Flexible and Open to Feedback: In the real world, you may not always have the luxury of getting **feedback** on every single idea. Be open to feedback from team members, stakeholders, and users, and be willing to pivot when necessary. Embrace the chaos of real-world ideation and see feedback as an opportunity for improvement.

For instance, a UX designer at a software company received feedback from users during usability testing that the product's registration process was too lengthy and complex, causing frustration and drop-offs. This feedback was collected from 15 users, including both new users and returning users, during a series of in-person usability sessions. The feedback not only highlighted a significant issue with the registration process but also convinced the stakeholders, including the product manager and development team, that simplification was necessary. The feedback was shared through a detailed usability testing report that included user quotes and data on drop-off rates. The evidence of user frustration and potential loss of users due to the complex registration process was compelling, and the stakeholders agreed that changes were needed. As a result, the design approach had to be pivoted, simplifying the registration process by reducing the number of steps and minimizing the required fields. This user feedback was instrumental in influencing the stakeholders' decision to prioritize and implement the changes, resulting in an improved onboarding experience for new users and a

30% increase in the conversion rate of the registration process. This experience reinforced the importance of gathering feedback directly from users to uncover usability issues and to advocate for changes with stakeholders for better user experience.

Be Inventive with Limited Resources: Ideation in the real world often requires being creative with limited time, budget, and resources. Look for creative ways to overcome constraints and come up with innovative solutions. For example, a UX team at a startup with a tight budget and limited resources used **guerrilla testing** to quickly gather feedback on their design ideas. They conducted **informal usability tests** with potential users in coffee shops and gathered valuable insights without incurring additional costs.

> **Rapid sketching** is a technique where you quickly draw rough, simple, and often incomplete sketches to generate ideas or communicate concepts. It's a way of visual brainstorming or ideation, where you can quickly capture your thoughts and explore different possibilities visually, without worrying about detailed or polished drawings. Rapid sketching can help you generate and communicate ideas efficiently, stimulate creativity, and facilitate collaboration among team members.

> **Brainwriting**, on the other hand, is a technique where ideas are generated in writing rather than verbally. It involves individuals writing down their ideas on paper, which are then shared and built upon by other team members. It allows for a structured and systematic approach to idea generation, where participants can contribute ideas independently and anonymously, without the pressure of speaking up in a group setting. Brainwriting encourages a diversity of ideas and can be used as a collaborative and efficient way to generate a large number of ideas in a relatively short amount

of time.

In the end, ideation in the real world is all about being creative, flexible, and efficient. Embrace the challenges, leverage techniques like design sprints and concept sketching, use pre-existing design systems, be open to feedback, and be creative with limited resources. With the right mindset and approach, you can come up with amazing ideas that meet deadlines and deliver high-quality results. Happy ideating!

From Sandcastles to Skyscrapers: The Reality of Wireframing

Wireframing is like a playground for UX designers, where we get to unleash our creativity and build the foundation for amazing user experiences. But just like a thrilling rollercoaster, wireframing in the real world comes with twists and turns, including tight deadlines, demanding stakeholders, and the occasional "creative" feedback that may or may not make sense. (We're looking at you, stakeholders who want to add a unicorn to their financial app!). Fear not, fellow designers! Here are some tips to navigate the reality of wireframing and come out victorious.

Communicate with stakeholders like a pro: When communicating design ideas to stakeholders, it's important to keep in mind that they may not be familiar with design jargon or technical terms. To effectively convey your ideas, use clear and visually-driven representations in your wireframes. This can include icons, symbols, illustrations, and other elements that help to clearly communicate design solutions that address the needs and goals of stakeholders. It's also important to avoid cluttering wireframes and to clearly show the potential interactions, including how the design solutions may adapt to different screen sizes.

Prioritize functionality over aesthetics (for now): It's tempting to get caught up in the visual details of wireframing, but in the real world, functionality is king. Focus on creating wireframes that clearly illustrate the flow and interaction of the user interface, ensuring that it is intuitive and efficient. You can always add the icing on the cake with aesthetics later.

> Striking the right **balance between aesthetics and functionality** can be challenging. While fonts, colors, and icons may not be a top priority in many projects at the early stages, there are cases where they play a crucial role. When designing a product for a specific audience, like people with dyslexia, selecting an accessible font becomes essential. In this scenario, the font choice goes beyond aesthetics and becomes a functional decision that defines the product's usability and accessibility.

Build a wireframe toolkit: Just like Batman has his utility belt, you can create your own wireframe toolkit. Include reusable design elements, such as buttons, forms, and icons, that align with your brand or project requirements. This will save you time and effort, allowing you to quickly iterate and meet tight deadlines with ease.

Embrace feedback (even the "creative" kind): Feedback from stakeholders and team members can sometimes be challenging, but it's an invaluable part of the design process. Be open to feedback, both positive and constructive, and use it to iterate and improve your wireframes. And remember, even the most unconventional feedback can sometimes lead to brilliant design solutions, so keep an open mind and stay adaptable.

Use real-world use cases: When creating wireframes, think about real-world scenarios and use cases that align with the goals of the project. Consider how different user personas might interact with the interface and design accordingly. This will help you create wireframes that are user-centric and aligned with the needs of your target audience.

Pro Tip. Collaborate with a product manager to generate a set of user stories based on real-world use cases.

Example User Story 1

As a registered user, I want to be able to reset my password so that I can securely regain access to my account if I forget my password.
A Sample Flow to Wireframe:

- User clicks on the "Forgot Password" link on the login page.
- User enters their registered email address.
- System sends a password reset link to the user's email.
- User receives the reset link and clicks on it.
- User is directed to a password reset page.
- User sets a new password.
- User receives confirmation of password reset and can now log in with the new password.

Example User Story 2

As a mobile app user, I want to be able to search for nearby restaurants based on my current location so that I can find and choose a restaurant that fits my preferences.
A Sample Flow to Wireframe:

- User opens the app and grants location access.
- User enters a search query or selects predefined filters for restaurant search.
- The app retrieves nearby restaurants based on the user's current location.
- User views a list of restaurants with relevant details, such as name, ratings, and distance.
- User selects a restaurant from the list for more details.
- User views additional information, such as menu, photos, and reviews, for the selected restaurant.
- User makes a decision and either adds the restaurant to favorites or proceeds to book a table or order food.

Wireframing in the real world can be challenging, but with the right mindset and strategies, you can conquer any design obstacle that comes your way. Embrace the thrilling ride, communicate effectively with stakeholders, prioritize functionality, build a wireframe toolkit, embrace feedback (even the "creative" kind), and use real-world use cases to guide your design decisions. Happy wireframing, fellow designers, and may your user experiences be delightful and your deadlines be conquerable!

Prototyping: Navigating the Fast Lane of Product Development with Resilience!

Welcome to the intricate world of prototyping, where managing numerous projects, sifting through a sea of feedback, adapting to constantly evolving requirements, and resolving stakeholder disputes can be like assembling a challenging puzzle with missing pieces. Although it may seem daunting, with a methodical and creative approach, you can gradually piece together the fragments of prototyping and construct a cohesive and polished MVP. To aid you in this endeavor, we offer actionable tips and relatable examples that can help you solve even the most vexing pieces of the prototyping puzzle with a lighthearted and resilient attitude.

> **MVP** stands for **Minimum Viable Product**. It is a concept used in product development that refers to the earliest version of a product or feature that can be released to users with the minimum set of features and functionalities required to solve a specific problem or address a specific need. The goal of an MVP is to quickly deliver a usable product to users, gather feedback, and iterate on subsequent versions based on user insights.
>
> From a UX perspective, an MVP is focused on delivering a product that provides a satisfactory user experience while minimizing unnecessary features or complexity. It typically includes the essential features that allow users to accomplish their goals,

while excluding non-essential features that can be added in later iterations. The UX design of an MVP should prioritize usability, simplicity, and efficiency to ensure that users can easily understand and use the product with minimal friction. The UX team plays a critical role in identifying the core user needs, designing the user interface, and conducting usability testing to validate the effectiveness of the MVP in meeting user expectations and solving their problems.

Challenge #1: Feature Creep Frenzy

As you gather feedback from stakeholders and users, you may face the challenge of feature creep, where every review seems to add yet another missing feature or forgotten workflow to the product. It can feel like a never-ending cycle of additions, modifications, and changes, leading to a bloated product that deviates from the original MVP vision.

To overcome this challenge, prioritize features and workflows based on their importance and alignment with the MVP vision. Have a clear roadmap and stick to it, resisting the temptation to add every suggested feature. Communicate with stakeholders about the trade-offs of feature creep and the need to maintain simplicity for the MVP. Use your expertise and creativity to balance feedback with the product's overall vision and keep feature creep in check!

> *Imagine you're a UX designer tasked with creating a new note-taking app. Some suggest adding voice recording, others suggest adding image attachments, and others want to integrate the app with social media platforms.*

Challenge #2: Simplifying in the Face of Complexity

Prototyping can involve complex systems and interactions, and keeping things simple and user-friendly can be a daunting task. It's easy to get caught up in the details and lose sight of the bigger picture, leading to a confusing and overwhelming product.

To overcome this challenge, focus on the product's core value proposition and the key user tasks. Streamline workflows, eliminate unnecessary steps, and simplify interactions to ensure a smooth user experience. Test the product with real users to identify pain points and areas for simplification. Embrace the mantra of "less is more" and strive for simplicity while maintaining usability and functionality!

> *A note-taking app may initially be designed with numerous features, such as formatting options, advanced search functions, and note-sharing capabilities. However, after testing the app with real users, the team may discover that many users find these additional features to be overwhelming and unnecessary. To simplify the app and improve the user experience, the team may decide to eliminate some of these features and streamline the workflow to focus on the core value proposition of the app: taking and organizing notes quickly and efficiently. Additionally, to further simplify the user experience, the app could automate certain tasks such as saving notes, instead of requiring the user to click a "save" button every time they make a change. This would not only eliminate the need for an extra click but also reduce the risk of the user accidentally losing their work.*

Challenge #3: Managing Stakeholder Expectations

Stakeholders often have different perspectives, priorities, and expectations when it comes to the product's features and functionalities. Managing conflicting stakeholder feedback and disagreements can be challenging and impact the product's direction.

To overcome this challenge, establish clear communication channels with stakeholders and set expectations early in the prototyping process. Align stakeholders on the MVP vision and objectives, and involve them in the decision-making process. Use data and user feedback to support your design decisions and justify trade-offs. Be diplomatic and tactful in managing stakeholder feedback, and find common ground to keep the project moving forward!

> *Let's continue with the example of the note-taking app that has multiple stakeholders involved in its development. The marketing team wants the app to be visually appealing and trendy, while the development team wants to focus on functionality and performance. The product manager wants the app to have a unique feature that sets it apart from competitors.*
>
> *To overcome this challenge, UX designers must establish clear communication channels with all stakeholders, ensuring they understand the MVP vision and objectives. It is essential to involve them in the decision-making process, gather feedback, and use data to support design decisions. UX designers must also be diplomatic and tactful in managing stakeholder feedback, considering everyone's perspective while ensuring the app's overall success.*
>
> *For example, in the case of our note-taking app, the UX designer could create multiple design options to address different stakeholder feedback. They could then present these options to stakeholders, outlining the benefits and drawbacks of each. By involving stakeholders and using data to support design decisions, UX designers can manage stakeholder expectations while ensuring the app's usability, functionality, and success.*

So there you have it, fellow UX designers! Navigate the fast lane of product development with playful resilience by managing feature creep, simplifying complexity, and handling stakeholder expectations with finesse. With strategic prioritization, simplicity in design, effective communication, and a resilient attitude, you'll overcome these challenges and create successful prototypes that stay true to the MVP vision!

Testing, Testing, 1-2-3...

Congratulations, you've finally made it to the testing phase of the UX process. However, in the real world, testing can often feel like a race against time. Deadlines are looming, budgets are tight, and getting actual users to participate can feel like an impossible feat. But fear not, we're here to help you navigate the rocky terrain of testing with limited resources.

First up, let's talk about **heuristic evaluation**. This technique involves having a group of experts evaluate your design against a set of established principles or heuristics. It's not as good as actual user testing, but it can still provide valuable feedback and help identify potential usability issues.

> **Heuristic evaluations** are a method used by usability experts to assess the user-friendliness of a product, like a website or app. They use a checklist of rules or principles, called heuristics, to

systematically evaluate the product for potential usability issues. These issues could include confusing navigation, unclear labels, inconsistent design, and more. The evaluator then provides feedback to improve the product's usability. Heuristic evaluations are typically conducted in the early stages of product development to catch and address problems before the product is launched to users, ensuring a better user experience.

Another option is an **expert review**, where you have a subject matter expert in your industry review your design. This can be especially helpful if you're designing for a niche audience or dealing with complex subject matter.

Expert review is a usability evaluation method that involves a single usability expert assessing a user interface based on their expertise. The expert evaluates the interface using various techniques such as cognitive walkthroughs, usability testing, and heuristics evaluations. Unlike heuristic evaluation, expert review does not involve a group of evaluators assessing the interface against a predefined set of usability principles. The main advantage of expert review is that it allows for a holistic evaluation of the user experience, as the expert can use their expertise to identify potential issues that may not be detected through other evaluation methods.

Finally, **guerrilla testing** can be a great way to get quick and dirty feedback on your design. This involves conducting informal testing with anyone who happens to be nearby, like friends, family members, or even strangers at a coffee shop. It's not the most scientific method, but it can provide valuable insights and help you identify potential issues that you might not have noticed otherwise.

So, even if you don't have the luxury of extensive user testing, there are still ways to get valuable feedback and improve your design. Just remember to keep an open mind, be flexible, and don't be afraid to try unconventional methods.

How to Play Picasso (Even if You're Not an Artist): A Guide to Visual Design

In the professional world, visual design is a critical stage where we bring wireframes to life by creating visually appealing interfaces. However, it's not just about aesthetics; it's about creating designs that are effective, user-friendly, and align with the stakeholders' vision.

In the real world, designers often encounter various constraints that can impact their creative freedom. These constraints include brand guidelines, accessibility requirements, device limitations, and industry-specific UI requirements. These factors can pose challenges while trying to create visually appealing designs that align with the brand's visual identity and meet user expectations.

> **Design is not just what it looks like and feels like. Design is how it works.**
>
> Steve Jobs, an American entrepreneur and co-founder of Apple Inc

Brand guidelines are a common constraint in visual design, providing a set of rules and standards for elements like colors, typography, and imagery. They ensure consistency and coherence across all design assets, but can also limit the options available to designers in terms of color palette or typography choices. This can pose a challenge for designers when brand guidelines prescribe colors that are commonly associated with certain meanings, such as red being associated with danger or warning. For example, brands like CNN, Equifax, or Verizon may have red as their primary color in their brand guidelines. Designers then face the task of finding creative ways to work around this constraint and create alternative colors for warnings and danger messages while still maintaining alignment with the brand's visual identity. It requires a delicate balance between adhering to brand guidelines and meeting user expectations of visual design patterns. Designers must think innovatively and resourcefully to come up with designs that stand out while still staying true to the brand's visual identity and the intended meaning of the design elements. This challenge calls for careful consideration of brand guidelines, user expectations, and the desired visual impact of the design to achieve an effective and visually appealing outcome.

Accessibility requirements are crucial constraints in visual design, as they ensure that designs are inclusive and accessible to a wide range of users. These requirements may impact color choices, font sizes, and other design elements.

For users with visual impairments, ensuring adequate color contrast is essential to improve readability. Alt text for images is necessary for users with visual or hearing impairments to understand the content. Designers may need to create different color modes, such as contrast mode, for apps and websites, and incorporate features like increased font size and larger icons to enhance accessibility.

Balancing accessibility requirements with other design considerations can be challenging, as designers need to ensure that the visual design remains inclusive while maintaining brand identity.

> *One good example of **balancing accessibility and aesthetics** in UX design is using color contrast appropriately. Accessibility standards may require a certain level of color contrast to ensure that content is legible for users with visual impairments. However, designers can still create visually appealing interfaces by carefully selecting color combinations that meet accessibility requirements while also aligning with the overall aesthetics of the design. For example, using contrasting colors that are visually appealing, but also meet the minimum contrast*

ratio requirements for accessibility can strike the right balance between aesthetics and accessibility.

Device requirements also pose constraints in visual design. Different devices, such as desktops, tablets, and mobile phones, have varying screen sizes and interaction patterns. Designers need to consider these constraints and create designs that are responsive and adaptable to different devices while maintaining visual consistency. Later on, we'll have a deeper dive into various devices and their unique visual design requirements.

In the wild world of visual design, **industry-specific UI requirements** can put some interesting constraints on designers. Take websites and apps, for example. In the healthcare industry, blue is often seen as the go-to color for trust and professionalism. So, if you're tasked with designing a website or app for a healthcare company and your brand guidelines dictate the use of blue as the main color, it can be a real puzzle to create a design that stands out from the countless other blue healthcare websites and apps out there. But watch out! Deviating from the expected blue might be met with some serious side-eye from customers who have come to associate blue with healthcare. It's like trying to navigate through a maze of blue without getting lost in the color palette! It's a challenge that requires some serious creativity, but hey, that's the colorful world of visual design for you!

To overcome these challenges, designers can adopt some practical approaches:

Understand and Collaborate with Brand and Industry: Designers need to thoroughly understand brand guidelines and industry-specific UI requirements while collaborating with brand and industry experts. This can involve discussions and clarifications on color choices, typography, and other design elements to find creative ways to work within the constraints while maintaining visual appeal.

Conduct User Research: Conducting user research, including usability testing and gathering feedback from the target audience, can help identify user expectations and preferences related to visual design. This information can guide designers in making informed decisions while adhering to brand guidelines and other constraints.

Experiment with Alternative Design Elements: Designers can experiment with alternative design elements, such as layout, imagery, and interactions, to create unique and visually appealing designs that still align with brand guidelines and industry expectations. This can involve creative use of whitespace, imagery, and typography to create a distinct look and feel while adhering to the constraints.

Stay Updated with Accessibility Standards: Keeping up-to-date with accessibility standards and best practices can help designers create inclusive designs that meet accessibility requirements while maintaining visual appeal. This can involve using accessible color palettes, providing alternative text for images, and using scalable fonts, among other considerations.

In summary, visual designers face various constraints in the real world. Overcoming these challenges requires a thorough understanding of the constraints, creative problem-solving, collaboration with brand and industry experts, and user-centered design approaches. By following these tips, designers can create visually appealing designs.

Development - The Wild West of UX

Development is where the rubber meets the road, and we learn the true meaning of teamwork. We hand off our pristine designs to the developers, and they take our visions and turn them into reality. But working with developers can feel like navigating the Wild West of UX. There are plenty of challenges to overcome, but with the right attitude and effective communication, we can make the journey together.

One of the biggest challenges is bridging the gap between design and development. Developers and designers speak different languages, and sometimes it can feel like we're talking past each other. Developers don't always understand the nuances of design, and designers don't always understand the technical constraints of development. This can lead to misunderstandings and delays, which can be frustrating for everyone involved.

Another challenge is responding to development questions about the designs. Sometimes developers will come to us with questions about how a particular element should work or how a feature should be implemented. We need to be able to answer these questions quickly and effectively to keep the project moving forward.

But perhaps the biggest challenge of all is dealing with developers who are resistant to change. They'll argue that the designs are impossible to implement or that it will take months to develop something that should only take hours. When we try to push back, they'll dismiss our concerns with a shrug and a "it works, doesn't it?"

To overcome these challenges, we need to be able to speak the language of development. We need to understand the basics of coding so that we can design for development and make it easier for developers to implement our designs. We also need to be able to explain the reasoning behind our designs in terms that developers can understand, highlighting the benefits of our design decisions.

Another strategy is to work closely with developers throughout the development process. By collaborating early and often, we can catch potential issues before they become major roadblocks. We can also come up with alternative solutions on the fly, so that we can make changes quickly without disrupting the development process.

Working with developers can be a challenging, but ultimately rewarding experience. By understanding their perspective, speaking their language, and collaborating closely throughout the development process, we can create delightful products that meet the needs of our users while staying within our project timelines. And who knows, we might even earn the respect of our developer colleagues along the way!

Surviving the Post-Launch Apocalypse

Congratulations! You've launched your product, and now the real fun begins. Brace yourself for a barrage of user feedback, some of which may be helpful, and some of which may make you question your life choices. The UX team must be prepared to listen and respond to all feedback while resisting the urge to scream into the void.

In addition to the feedback frenzy, the UX team must stay ahead of the latest design trends and technologies. It's a race against time as new tech emerges faster than a toddler's tantrum. If you fall behind, your product risks becoming a relic of the past, like a VHS tape or a Blockbuster store.

But that's not all! You must also measure the success of your product post-launch through KPIs. And we all know how fun it is to decipher those analytics reports. It's like trying to solve a Rubik's Cube blindfolded while balancing a spoon on your nose.

KPI stands for **Key Performance Indicator**. It's a way to measure how well someone or something is doing. Imagine you're playing a video game, and you want to see how good you are at it. You might look at your score or how many levels you've completed. Those are like KPIs because they help you see how well you're doing in the game. In real life, businesses and organizations also use KPIs to measure how well they're doing in achieving their goals. Just like in a video game, KPIs can help them keep track of their progress and make improvements if needed.

Lastly, the UX team must collaborate with other teams within the organization to ensure that the product is being promoted and supported correctly. This includes working with the marketing team, whose creativity may make your brain hurt, and customer support, who deal with customers all day, every day. Bless their souls.

To tackle these challenges, the UX team should establish a process for collecting and analyzing user feedback. Just make sure to have plenty of coffee on hand. The team should also attend industry events and read design blogs, but let's be real, they'll probably end up binging Netflix instead.

Feedback collection and analysis involve gathering feedback from various sources to understand what people think about a product, service, or experience, and using that feedback to make improvements. There are several options for feedback collection and analysis, such as online surveys using tools like Google Forms or SurveyMonkey, feedback forms on websites or apps where users can provide feedback directly, monitoring social media for comments and mentions, in-app feedback mechanisms in mobile apps or software, and using customer feedback management platforms like Medallia or Qualtrics to collect and analyze feedback from different sources. These tools can help organizations better understand customer preferences, identify areas for improvement, and make data-driven decisions to enhance their products or services.

Establishing KPIs will help measure the success of the product post-launch, but let's not forget to celebrate the little wins along the way, like fixing a typo or finding a bug before the users do.

Communication and collaboration are key. So, take a deep breath, and remember, you're all in this together. It's like a team-building exercise, but with fewer trust falls and more gifs. Surviving the post-launch apocalypse as a UX team can be a challenge, but with a positive outlook and a lot of caffeine, you can navigate through the chaos and emerge victorious.

* * *

Chapter 2: Building Your UX Arsenal

Welcome to the UX battlefield, where the skills you wield are the key to victory in the war against bad user experiences! In this chapter, we'll equip you with the essential skills you need to navigate the real-life challenges of UX design and emerge triumphant in your quest for design success.

Just like a seasoned warrior needs battle-tested skills, a UX designer needs a practical set of skills to tackle the complexities of real-life UX projects. From conducting user research in the field to wireframing, prototyping, and visual design in the trenches of everyday work situations, we'll cover it all with a touch of humor and a dash of wit.

As a UX designer, you'll need to be proficient in understanding user needs, creating effective user flows, crafting engaging interactions, conducting usability testing, and incorporating feedback into your designs. You'll also need to have a keen eye for visual design, understanding how to use color, typography, and layout to create aesthetically pleasing and functional interfaces.

In addition to technical skills, soft skills are equally important in UX design. Communication and collaboration skills are vital for working with cross-functional teams, stakeholders, and clients. Problem-solving and critical thinking skills will help you tackle complex design challenges and come up with innovative solutions. Empathy and understanding of human behavior are crucial for designing experiences that are user-centric and meaningful.

So, whether you're a seasoned UX veteran looking to sharpen your skills for the battlefield of real-life projects, or a fresh recruit just starting out, this chapter will be your guide to building a formidable UX arsenal that's ready for the challenges of the real world. So gear up, and get ready to conquer the user experience design landscape with skills that are battle-tested, practical, and tailored for success in real-life work situations. Let's charge into the fray and achieve UX victory!

The Ultimate Arsenal of UX Designer Skills

Imagine a UX designer as a skilled conductor, orchestrating a symphony of elements to create harmonious and delightful user experiences. Like a maestro, a successful UX designer possesses a diverse set of skills and talents that they skillfully wield to create masterpieces in the form of digital products and services.

> **UX Design Skills** are core competencies applicable across various specialties.

Just like a **tuning fork** helps a musician find the right pitch, **user research** is the foundation for a UX designer. They use various methods to understand the needs, preferences, and behaviors of their target users, ensuring that their designs are in tune with user expectations.

Information architecture is like **the sheet music** that guides the conductor and musicians. A UX designer creates clear and organized information architectures, mapping out the structure and flow of the user experience, so that users can easily navigate and find what they need.

Interaction design is like the **melodic phrasing** that adds rhythm and flow to the user experience. A skilled UX designer designs intuitive and seamless interactions, ensuring that users can smoothly interact with the product or service.

Visual design is like the **symphony** of colors, shapes, and visual elements that bring a design to life. A UX designer creates visually appealing and aesthetically pleasing designs that engage and captivate users, creating a memorable experience.

Prototyping is like a **rehearsal** where the UX designer tests and refines their design before the final performance. They create prototypes to gather feedback, iterate on their designs, and ensure that the user experience is polished and refined.

Usability testing is like receiving **feedback** from the audience during a performance. A UX designer conducts usability tests to gather insights from real users, uncovering any issues or areas of improvement in the design.

Collaborative skills are like a **conductor's baton**, leading and guiding the team to create a cohesive and harmonious design. A successful UX designer collaborates with cross-functional team members, such as developers, product managers, and stakeholders, to align the design with the overall product vision.

Communication skills are like the **interpretation** a conductor brings to a musical piece. A UX designer communicates their design decisions effectively to team members, clients, and stakeholders, ensuring that everyone is on the same page and working towards a shared vision.

Accessibility is like creating **inclusive melodies** that cater to all users, regardless of their abilities. A UX designer ensures that their designs are accessible and usable by a diverse range of users, including those with disabilities, ensuring inclusivity.

Project management skills are like a **symphony conductor**, overseeing the entire UX design process from start to finish. A UX designer manages timelines, resources, and deliverables, ensuring that the design project progresses smoothly and is completed successfully.

Agile methodology is like a **dynamic orchestra**, where the UX designer adapts and iterates their design based on feedback and changing project requirements. They collaborate with the team in an agile environment, adjusting their design approach as needed to keep the project in tune with user needs and business goals.

Front-end development is like a **versatile instrument** that a UX designer can play to bring their designs to life. With front-end development skills, a UX designer can create interactive prototypes, implement responsive designs, and collaborate with developers to ensure that the final product meets the intended user experience.

Content strategy is like the **lyrics** that accompany the melodies of a design. A UX designer crafts thoughtful and meaningful content strategies that align with the overall user experience, ensuring that the content is engaging, informative, and easy to understand.

User testing is like a **sound check** before a performance, where a UX designer validates their design with real users. They conduct user testing sessions to gather feedback and insights, making necessary adjustments to the design to ensure that it meets the needs and expectations of users.

Data analysis is like a **musical score** that provides insights and guidance for a UX designer. They analyze data from user research, usability testing, and other sources to inform their design decisions, ensuring that their design is evidence-based and data-driven.

Keeping up with **emerging technologies** is like being a **musical innovator**, exploring new techniques, tools, and design patterns. A UX designer stays updated with the latest trends in UX design and technology, incorporating innovative solutions into their designs to create cutting-edge user experiences.

Empathy and human-centered design are like the **heartbeat** of the UX designer. They put themselves in the shoes of the users, understanding their emotions, motivations, and needs, and design with empathy to create meaningful and user-centric experiences.

Problem-solving is like a **creative improvisation** where the UX designer finds innovative solutions to design challenges. They analyze complex problems, think critically, and come up with creative and practical solutions to create the best user experience possible.

Attention to detail is like the **fine musical notes** that make up a beautiful melody. A successful UX designer pays meticulous attention to every detail of their design, from the placement of buttons to the spacing of text, ensuring a visually appealing and polished experience.

Flexibility is like a **musical ensemble**, where the UX designer adapts to different design projects, users, and business requirements. They are flexible in their approach, open to feedback and changes, and can pivot their design direction as needed to meet project goals.

User advocacy is like the role of a **maestro** who champions the needs and interests of the users. A UX designer serves as the advocate for the users throughout the design process, ensuring that their voice is heard, their needs are considered, and their experience is prioritized, just as a maestro leads and directs the orchestra to create a harmonious performance.

Simplicity is like a **catchy melody** that resonates with users. A UX designer strives for simplicity in their design, creating a clear, easy-to-use, and intuitive user interface that users can quickly understand and interact with, resulting in a memorable and enjoyable user experience.

Time management is like a **well-timed rhythm** that keeps the UX design process on track. A UX designer manages their time effectively, prioritizes tasks, and meets deadlines to ensure that the project progresses smoothly and is delivered on time.

Continuous learning is like a **never-ending symphony**, where the UX designer constantly expands their knowledge and skills. They stay updated with the latest design trends, UX research methods, and industry best practices, and strive for continuous improvement in their craft.

Resilience is like a **musical encore**, where the UX designer faces challenges and setbacks with determination and perseverance. They learn from failures, iterate on their designs, and bounce back stronger, ensuring that the final design is a resounding success.

Passion for UX design is like a **creative inspiration** that drives the UX designer to create remarkable experiences. It fuels their creativity, motivates them to go the extra mile, and instills a deep sense of pride and satisfaction in their work.

Just like a conductor skillfully conducts a symphony, a successful UX designer possesses a **symphony of skills**, ranging from user research and information architecture to interaction design, visual design, prototyping, usability testing, collaboration, communication, accessibility, project management, agility, innovation, empathy, problem-solving, attention to detail, flexibility, time management, continuous learning, resilience, and a passion for UX design. It is the harmonious combination of these skills that allows a UX designer to create truly remarkable user experiences that delight and engage users, leaving a lasting impression.

UX Design Specialties: Exploring the Diverse World of User Experience Design

Welcome to the exciting realm of UX design, where we create digital experiences that delight users and make their lives easier. As UX designers, we have a wide range of specialties to choose from, each with its unique flavors of creativity, methods, and expertise.

From understanding user behavior to crafting beautiful interfaces and making digital products accessible to all, there's something for everyone in the world of UX design. Think of it like a buffet of design superpowers, with each specialty offering its own set of skills and techniques.

So, get ready to embark on a thrilling adventure as we dive into the secrets of these UX design specialties. Whether you're interested in research, visual design, writing, or strategy, there's a world of possibilities to explore in UX wonderland. Let's unleash our enthusiasm and start the UX-plore!

> **UX Design Specialties** are specific areas within UX design that require specialized knowledge.

Interaction Designer

Welcome to the world of Interaction Design, where we specialize in creating seamless and efficient interactions for digital products. Our tools include wireframing, prototyping, and user testing to craft delightful user experiences.

Our goal is to ensure that users can easily navigate, interact, and accomplish tasks in the digital world. We carefully design intuitive interactions that leave users wanting more, just like a well-crafted user interface that enhances the overall user experience.

As the experts in digital interactions, we blend together the right ingredients to create a symphony of interactions that make the user journey smooth and enjoyable.

Daily tasks of an Interaction Designer may include

- **Wireframing:** Creating wireframes or low-fidelity prototypes to map out the interactions and flow of a digital product. This involves sketching out rough layouts, defining interaction patterns, and considering user interactions in different scenarios.
- **Prototyping:** Building interactive prototypes using tools like Sketch, Figma, or InVision to test and refine the interactions. This may involve creating clickable mockups, simulating user interactions, and gathering feedback from stakeholders or users.
- **Interaction Patterns:** Designing and implementing reusable interaction patterns, such as buttons, forms, menus, and navigation, that provide a consistent and familiar experience for users across different parts of the product or application.

These tasks require a deep understanding of user behavior, usability principles, and technical feasibility to create interactions that enhance the overall user experience. Interaction Designers work closely with UX/UI Designers, developers, and stakeholders to ensure that interactions align with the overall product vision and meet the needs of both the users and the business.

Visual Designer

Welcome to the world of Visual Design, where we specialize in crafting visually delightful experiences for users. Our tools include graphic design software, prototyping, and a keen eye for aesthetics to create visually appealing and user-friendly digital products.

As visual designers, we carefully select the right ingredients of layout, typography, color schemes, and brand identity to create visually engaging interfaces that captivate users. We understand the importance of aesthetics in creating a memorable user experience, and we strive to balance usability with visual appeal.

Daily tasks of a Visual Designer may include

- **Creating visual assets:** Designing icons, buttons, illustrations, and other visual elements that are used in the digital product to enhance the user interface and create a visually appealing experience.
- **Crafting layouts:** Creating visually balanced and responsive layouts that optimize the use of space, typography, and color to guide users through the interface and facilitate their interactions.
- **Branding and identity:** Ensuring consistency with the brand identity of the product or company, including color schemes, typography, and

visual elements, to create a cohesive and memorable visual experience.

- **Prototyping and testing:** Building interactive prototypes to test and refine the visual design, and gathering feedback from stakeholders or users to make improvements and iterate on the design.
- **Collaborating with UX/UI Designers:** Working closely with UX/UI Designers, developers, and stakeholders to ensure that the visual design aligns with the overall user experience and product vision.

Visual Designers play a crucial role in creating visually appealing and engaging digital experiences that leave a lasting impression on users. We strive to create interfaces that not only look good but also enhance usability and provide a seamless user experience. Join us in the world of visual design and let's create visually delightful experiences together!

Information Architect

Welcome to the world of Information Architecture, where we specialize in creating well-organized and user-friendly digital products. Just like a skilled chef, we curate the perfect recipe of information, ensuring that users can easily digest and navigate through the digital experience without feeling overwhelmed.

Our toolkit includes techniques like card sorting, content mapping, and information hierarchy, which allow us to create a structured information architecture that guides users through the digital experience. We label and categorize with precision, ensuring that users can understand and access the information with ease.

Daily tasks of an Information Architect may include

- **Content organization:** Curating and organizing the information in a digital product, ensuring that it is structured in a logical and user-friendly manner, and aligns with the overall content strategy.
- **User research:** Conducting user research to understand user needs and preferences, and using that information to inform the information architecture of the digital product.
- **Navigation design:** Designing intuitive navigation systems, including menus, filters, and search functionalities, that allow users to easily find and access the information they need.
- **Collaboration with stakeholders:** Working closely with content creators, UX/UI designers, developers, and other stakeholders to ensure that the information architecture aligns with the overall user experience and product vision.

Information Architects play a critical role in creating digital products that are easy to navigate and understand, providing users with a seamless and satisfying experience. With a deep understanding of user needs, content strategy, and usability principles, we design the perfect blend of information that helps users find what they need efficiently.

If you have a passion for organizing and structuring information with finesse, come join us in the world of Information Architecture and let's create digital experiences that are intuitive and user-friendly!

Card sorting is a technique where people group and categorize information on cards based on their own understanding, helping designers better organize information for user-friendly products or services.

Content mapping is the process of visually outlining and organizing content in a structured way, helping to create a clear and organized structure for the presentation of information or content within a product or service.

Information hierarchy refers to the organization and arrangement of content or information in a product or service, ensuring that it is presented in a clear and logical way, with important or relevant information prioritized and easily accessible, while less important or secondary information is appropriately nested or displayed.

User Researcher

Just like a skilled detective, user researchers diligently investigate the preferences and needs of users. We delve deep into their behaviors, motivations, and feedback, carefully analyzing the information to inform the design process.

Using techniques such as interviews, surveys, usability testing, and ethnographic research, we gather data that serves as our palette of insights. We meticulously analyze and interpret the data, extracting valuable information that guides the design team in creating delightful experiences for users.

We work closely with the design team, providing them with our expert feedback and insights, much like a detective would provide clues to solve a case. We ensure that the design decisions are grounded in user needs, preferences, and behaviors, creating designs that are truly user-centric and satisfying to the target audience.

Daily tasks of a User Researcher may include

- **Research planning:** Developing research plans, including defining research objectives, selecting appropriate methods, and recruiting participants.
- **Data collection:** Conducting interviews, surveys, usability tests, and other research methods to gather user insights.
- **Data analysis:** Analyzing and interpreting research data, identifying patterns, trends, and opportunities for improving the user experience.
- **Reporting and communication:** Presenting research findings to the design team and other stakeholders, and collaborating with them to integrate user insights into the design process.

User researchers play a crucial role in informing the design process and ensuring that the final product meets the needs and preferences of the target users. With our keen understanding of user behaviors and motivations, we help create user-centric designs that are effective and engaging.

If you have a knack for uncovering the preferences and needs of users, come join us in the world of user research and let's create designs that are truly user-centric and satisfying!

Accessibility Designer

Just like an experienced architect who designs buildings with accessibility in mind, accessibility designers create digital products that are inclusive and accommodating to all users, regardless of their abilities or disabilities.

We follow established accessibility standards and guidelines, such as the Web Content Accessibility Guidelines (WCAG), to ensure that our designs meet the needs of diverse users. We use techniques such as providing alternative text for images, adding captions to multimedia content, and ensuring keyboard navigation is seamless, making our designs accessible and usable for everyone.

We pay attention to the smallest details, just like an architect considers accessibility features in the layout of a building. We ensure that our designs are inclusive, considerate, and thoughtful so that all users can have a positive experience while using digital products.

Daily tasks of an Accessibility Designer may include

- **Reviewing and implementing accessibility standards:** Ensuring that digital products meet the requirements of accessibility standards and guidelines, such as WCAG, and implementing necessary design changes.
- **Conducting accessibility audits:** Evaluating existing digital products for accessibility issues and recommending solutions for improvement.
- **Collaborating with design and development teams:** Working closely with design and development teams to incorporate accessibility principles into the design and development process.
- **User testing:** Conducting usability testing with users with disabilities to gather feedback and insights on the accessibility of digital products.

Accessibility designers play a crucial role in creating digital products that are inclusive and accommodating to all users, regardless of their abilities. We strive to ensure that everyone can access and use digital products effectively and enjoyably, without facing any barriers.

If you have a passion for creating inclusive experiences and ensuring that digital products are accessible to all, come join us in the world of accessibility design and let's create designs that are inclusive and accommodating for every user!

Mobile Designer

Mobile designers specialize in creating user experiences for the small screens of smartphones and tablets, much like a skilled pilot who navigates through changing weather conditions to ensure a smooth flight.

We understand the unique constraints and opportunities of mobile devices, including touch interfaces and on-the-go usage. We create designs that are optimized for mobile use, ensuring that users can seamlessly interact with digital products on their handheld devices.

Just like a pilot who adjusts their flight plan based on changing weather conditions, we create responsive and adaptive designs that provide consistent user experiences across different mobile devices and screen sizes. We carefully consider the user's context and behavior, and create intuitive and efficient interactions that are tailored for mobile usage.

Daily tasks of a Mobile Designer may include

- **Designing mobile user interfaces:** Creating visually appealing and functional user interfaces for mobile applications and websites, taking into consideration the unique constraints of mobile devices.
- **Conducting user research:** Understanding user behavior and preferences on mobile devices through research techniques such as user interviews and usability testing.
- **Creating interactive prototypes:** Building interactive prototypes to test and validate design concepts, ensuring that they work seamlessly on mobile devices.
- **Collaborating with development teams:** Working closely with development teams to implement mobile designs and provide guidance on best practices for mobile user experience.

Mobile designers play a crucial role in creating enjoyable and efficient user experiences on mobile devices. We strive to create designs that are visually appealing, functional, and optimized for mobile usage, so that users can easily navigate and interact with digital products on their smartphones and tablets.

If you have a passion for crafting user experiences that fit in the palm of your hand, come join us in the world of mobile design and let's create mobile experiences that users can enjoy on the go!

Gamification Designer

Gamification designers specialize in using game design principles to enhance non-gaming contexts, creating interactive and engaging experiences that are as captivating as a thrilling adventure!

Just like a skilled explorer mapping out a new territory, gamification designers use techniques such as points, badges, leaderboards, and challenges to create immersive experiences that motivate users to take action, achieve goals, and form habits.

We leverage the psychological principles of motivation, reward, and feedback to create experiences that keep users coming back for more, just like how an adventurous traveler can't resist exploring another unknown path.

Whether it's conquering tasks, unlocking achievements, or climbing the leaderboard, our gamification designs add an extra layer of excitement and motivation to digital products.

Daily tasks of a Gamification Designer may include

- **Designing game mechanics:** Creating game mechanics such as points, levels, rewards, and challenges to motivate users and drive desired behaviors in non-gaming contexts.
- **Creating interactive experiences:** Designing interactive experiences that encourage users to engage, interact, and participate in the gamified elements of a digital product.
- **Conducting user research:** Understanding user preferences and behaviors through research techniques such as user interviews and usability testing to inform the design of gamification elements.
- **Evaluating and optimizing designs:** Analyzing user data and feedback to evaluate the effectiveness of gamification designs and making iterative improvements to enhance user engagement.

Gamification designers play a crucial role in creating captivating user experiences that keep users engaged and motivated. We strive to create designs that are immersive, rewarding, and tailored to the needs and preferences of the target audience.

If you have a passion for using game design principles to create engaging experiences, come join us in the world of gamification design and let's embark on an exciting journey of designing immersive and motivating user experiences!

Voice User Interface (VUI) Designer

Voice User Interface (VUI) designers are like inventors, pioneering new ways for users to interact with digital products using the power of voice commands.

Similar to how inventors come up with innovative solutions to problems, VUI designers create conversational interfaces that revolutionize the way users interact with technology by leveraging the power of voice recognition, natural language processing, and conversational design.

Just like how inventors constantly experiment and iterate to refine their inventions, VUI designers continuously refine their designs through user research, testing, and optimization to create intuitive and seamless voice-enabled experiences.

Daily tasks of a VUI Designer may include

- **Inventing new interaction paradigms:** Coming up with new ways for users to interact with digital products using their voice, such as designing novel conversational flows and voice commands that are intuitive and efficient.
- **Creating interactive experiences:** Designing voice-enabled experiences that respond to users' voice commands in a meaningful and engaging way, providing relevant and contextual responses, and creating a conversational flow that feels natural and enjoyable.
- **Conducting user research:** Understanding users' needs, preferences, and behaviors through research techniques such as user interviews, surveys, and usability testing to inform the design of voice-enabled elements and optimize user interactions.
- **Iterating and optimizing designs:** Analyzing user data and feedback to evaluate the effectiveness of VUI designs and making iterative improvements to enhance user satisfaction and engagement, just like how inventors iterate on their prototypes to make them better.

VUI designers are like inventors, pushing the boundaries of technology and designing interactions that are intuitive, convenient, and tailored to the needs of users. We strive to create voice-enabled experiences that are innovative, user-friendly, and enhance the way users interact with digital products.

If you have a passion for inventing new ways for users to interact with technology using the power of voice, come join us in the world of VUI design and let's invent exciting and immersive user experiences together!

Now, you might be thinking, "Wait, gamification and voice user interface design? Are those real UX design specialties or are you just pulling my leg?" Well, believe it or not, these are indeed real and emerging specialties in the world of UX design. As technology evolves and user behaviors change, UX designers are constantly exploring new ways to create innovative and engaging experiences for users. And yes, sometimes they even draw inspiration from the world of games and science fiction!

Let's take a closer look at these emerging specialties

Gamification Design: Turning mundane tasks into epic quests!

Imagine checking your email and instead of seeing a boring list of messages, you're greeted with a virtual treasure chest that you can unlock by completing tasks. Or picture yourself navigating through a website that rewards you with points and badges for each completed action, and you can level up to unlock special features. That's the magic of gamification design!

Gamification designers are like wizards who sprinkle a bit of pixie dust on digital products to make them more exciting and engaging. They use game design principles and mechanics, such as points, rewards, and challenges, to transform mundane tasks into epic quests that users are motivated to complete. They create experiences that tap into our human desire for competition, achievement, and rewards, making even the most mundane tasks feel like a fun and rewarding adventure.

So, the next time you find yourself eagerly checking your email just to unlock a virtual treasure chest, you'll know who to thank - the gamification designers who turned your inbox into a magical world of adventure!

> ## If you can design one thing, you can design everything.
>
> Massimo Vignelli, Italian graphic, industrial and interior designer

Voice User Interface (VUI) Design: Talking to technology like it's a BFF!

Remember the days when talking to inanimate objects was considered strange behavior? Well, not anymore! Thanks to voice-enabled devices like smart speakers and virtual assistants, we now talk to technology like it's our best friend forever (BFF).

VUI designers are like language wizards who create conversational interfaces that understand our voice commands and respond like a friendly chat. They consider factors such as natural language processing, voice recognition, and conversational flow to create intuitive and seamless interactions with technology. They make sure that our virtual BFFs understand us even when we mumble, stutter, or use slang, and respond with wit and charm.

With VUI design, we can now have meaningful conversations with our devices, from asking for the weather forecast to telling a joke or playing our favorite song. It's like having a personal assistant who's always there to chat and entertain us, without ever getting bored or annoyed. Who knew talking to technology could be so much fun?

Unlocking Your UX Design Potential: Discovering Your Specialization in the Realm of User Experience Design

When it comes to finding your specialization in digital design, it's essential to consider your interests, strengths, and career goals. Are you passionate about creating visually stunning interfaces? Visual design may be your calling. Do you enjoy understanding user behavior and conducting research? User research or information architecture may be the right fit. Are you drawn to creating immersive and engaging experiences? Gamification design or VUI design may be your cup of tea. By identifying your strengths and interests, you can narrow down your options and embark on a journey to specialize in a specific area of digital design.

It's also crucial to gain practical experience and continuously learn and grow in your chosen specialty. Keep yourself updated with the latest trends, tools, and techniques in your specialization, and seek opportunities to apply your skills through real-world projects or collaborations. Build a portfolio that showcases your expertise in your chosen specialty, and network with other professionals in the field to gain insights and learn from their experiences.

The field of UX design offers a wide range of specializations that cater to different interests, skills, and passions. It's essential to find your own UX specialization based on your strengths, interests, and career goals. Here are some tips to help you in your quest:

Reflect on your passions and skills: Consider what aspects of UX design you are most passionate about and where your skills align. Are you more interested in user research, interaction design, visual design, information architecture, UX writing, or another area? Assess your strengths and interests to identify the specialization that resonates with you the most.

Gain experience in different areas: Don't be afraid to explore different areas of UX design and gain experience in various specializations. Try working on different projects, collaborating with different teams, and learning different tools and techniques. This will help you broaden your skill set and gain insights into different aspects of UX design, which can eventually guide you towards your specialization.

Seek mentorship and guidance: Connect with experienced UX professionals and seek their mentorship and guidance. Learn from their experiences, seek advice, and ask questions about different specializations. Their insights can help you better understand the nuances of different areas of UX design and make informed decisions about your specialization.

Keep learning and growing: UX design is a constantly evolving field, and it's important to keep learning and growing to stay relevant. Stay updated with the latest industry trends, tools, and techniques. Take courses, attend workshops, read books, and participate in communities and forums to enhance your skills and knowledge in your chosen specialization.

Build a portfolio: As you gain experience in different areas of UX design, it's crucial to build a portfolio that showcases your skills and expertise in your chosen specialization. Your portfolio should include relevant projects, case studies, and examples of your work that demonstrate your proficiency in your specialization. Having a strong portfolio will not only help you showcase your skills to potential employers or clients but also establish your credibility as a specialist in your chosen field.

Network and collaborate: Networking is an essential aspect of any profession, including UX design. Connect with other UX professionals, join industry events, attend meetups, and participate in online communities related to your specialization. Collaborate with other designers, developers, researchers, and business strategists to expand your knowledge and gain new perspectives. Building a strong professional network can open up opportunities for mentorship, collaboration, and career growth in your chosen specialization.

Stay adaptable and open to learning: UX design is a field that is constantly evolving, and it's important to stay adaptable and open to learning. Keep yourself updated with the latest advancements, emerging technologies, and industry trends in your specialization. Be willing to learn new tools, techniques, and methodologies to stay ahead in your field. The ability to adapt and learn is crucial for professional growth and success in any specialization.

Remember, finding your specialization is not a one-time decision, but rather an ongoing process of exploration, learning, and growth. Don't be afraid to experiment, try new things, and evolve as a designer. Your specialization may change over time as you gain experience and discover new interests, and that's perfectly normal. The key is to stay curious, passionate, and committed to honing your skills and becoming a master in your chosen digital design specialty.

Becoming a UX Unicorn: Unlocking the Mythical World of Multidisciplinary UX Design

In the ever-evolving field of user experience (UX) design, professionals who possess a diverse skill set and expertise in multiple areas are often referred to as "UX Unicorns." These elusive creatures are highly sought-after in the industry due to their ability to not only excel in traditional UX activities such as research, testing, and prototyping but also to design visually appealing user interfaces (UI) and even code front-end elements. In this section, we will explore who UX unicorns are and delve into the path of becoming one. From understanding the key traits and skills of a UX unicorn to learning practical tips and strategies, this section aims to demystify the concept of UX unicorns and provide guidance for those aspiring to become one.

Who are UX Unicorns?

UX unicorns are professionals who possess a unique blend of skills and expertise across different disciplines within the field of UX design. They are not limited to a single role or skill set, but rather have a holistic understanding of the entire UX design process. UX unicorns are known for their ability to handle various aspects of UX design, from research and testing to information architecture, wireframing/prototyping, UI design, and front-end development. They are well-versed in the principles of usability, accessibility, and visual design, and are capable of applying these principles effectively in their work. UX unicorns are also known for their adaptability, versatility, and problem-solving skills, allowing them to tackle complex design challenges with ease.

Traits and Skills of a UX Unicorn

- **Diverse Skill Set:** A UX unicorn possesses a wide range of skills across different areas of UX design. They are proficient in conducting user research, analyzing data, creating customer journeys, developing task flows, crafting information architecture, wireframing/prototyping, creating visually appealing UI designs, and coding front-end elements using HTML, CSS, and JavaScript.

- **Strong Design Thinking:** UX unicorns are skilled in applying design thinking principles to their work. They have a deep understanding of user-centered design, empathy for users, and the ability to identify and address user needs and pain points through their design solutions.
- **Adaptability:** UX unicorns are adaptable and flexible in their approach to design. They are open to feedback, willing to iterate and iterate on their designs based on user feedback, and are not afraid to step out of their comfort zones to learn and explore new techniques and tools.
- **Problem-solving Skills:** UX unicorns are excellent problem solvers. They have the ability to identify and address design challenges, find creative solutions to complex problems, and make informed design decisions based on research and data.
- **Collaboration:** UX unicorns are effective collaborators. They are skilled in working with cross-functional teams, including product managers, developers, and stakeholders, and are able to communicate their design decisions and rationale clearly to ensure a collaborative and cohesive UX design process.
- **Continuous Learning:** UX unicorns have a growth mindset and a thirst for learning. They are constantly staying updated with the latest trends, tools, and techniques in the field of UX design and investing in their professional development to enhance their skills and knowledge.

How to Become a UX Unicorn

Becoming a UX unicorn is a challenging but achievable goal for those who are willing to put in the effort and dedication. Here are some practical tips and strategies for aspiring UX unicorns:

- **Develop a Solid Foundation:** Start by building a strong foundation in UX design principles and methodologies. Acquire knowledge and skills in areas such as user research, usability testing, information architecture, wireframing/prototyping, UI design, and front-end development. Gain experience through internships, projects, and real-world applications to build a solid portfolio that showcases your diverse skill set.

- **Specialize in One or Two Areas:** While UX unicorns are known for their multidisciplinary skills, it's also important to specialize in one or two areas of UX design. This could be UI design, front-end development, or any other area that you are particularly interested in and passionate about. Develop expertise in those areas by continuously learning and practicing, and showcase your specialized skills in your portfolio.

- **Gain Real-world Experience:** Seek opportunities to work on real-world projects to gain practical experience. This could be through internships, freelance work, or personal projects. Real-world experience will not only help you build your skills but also provide you with valuable insights and exposure to different UX design scenarios.

- **Learn and Experiment with Tools and Technologies:** Stay updated with the latest tools and technologies used in UX design. Experiment with different prototyping tools, design software, and front-end development frameworks to broaden your skill set and stay relevant in the industry. Keep learning and adapting to new technologies as the field of UX design is constantly evolving.

- **Build a Strong Portfolio:** Your portfolio is your showcase of skills and expertise. Build a strong portfolio that demonstrates your ability to handle different aspects of UX design, from research and testing to UI design and front-end development. Include case studies that highlight your process, approach, and the impact of your designs on users.

- **Collaborate with Others:** Collaboration is a key aspect of UX design. Collaborate with cross-functional teams, work on group projects, and seek feedback from peers and mentors to improve your skills and learn from others. Collaborating with others will also help you understand different perspectives and approaches to UX design.

- **Continuously Improve and Update Your Skills:** UX design is a constantly evolving field, and it's important to continuously improve and update your skills. Stay curious, be open to feedback, and seek opportunities for learning and growth. Attend workshops, webinars, conferences, and other industry events to stay updated with the latest trends and best practices in UX design.

Becoming a UX unicorn requires a combination of technical skills, personality traits, and soft skills. Dedication, continuous learning, and practical experience are crucial. By developing a diverse skill set, you can excel in different aspects of UX design and thrive in this ever-evolving field. It takes time and effort, but with the right mindset, determination, creativity, empathy, and strong communication skills, you can unlock the mythical world of multidisciplinary UX design and become a sought-after UX professional.

* * *

Chapter 3: Balancing UX Design with Real-World Constraints

Welcome to the world of juggling - not the circus kind, but the art of balancing multiple balls in the air at once. As a UX designer in the real world, you're often tasked with juggling multiple priorities and constraints at the same time. It can feel overwhelming, but fear not my fellow jugglers - it's all about finding a balance.

Let's start with the first ball - **user needs**. In an ideal world, you'd have all the time in the world to gather insights and create a perfect design that meets every user's needs. But in reality, you might need to prioritize certain needs over others, or even compromise on some to meet business goals. It's a delicate balance, but one that can be achieved with careful consideration and communication with stakeholders.

The second ball is **resources**. Whether it's time, money, or manpower, resources are always limited in the real world. You might need to work within tight budgets or work with a small team. This can be frustrating, but it's also an opportunity to get creative and find innovative solutions that work within your constraints.

The third ball is **technology**. As a UX designer, you need to be familiar with the latest tools and technologies. But in the real world, you might not always have access to the latest and greatest. You might need to work with outdated systems or find workarounds to achieve your goals. Again, it's all about being flexible and finding solutions that work within your constraints.

And finally, the fourth ball is **time**. In school, you might have had all the time in the world to perfect your designs. But in the real world, time is often your biggest constraint. You might need to work within tight deadlines or prioritize certain tasks over others. It's all about finding ways to work efficiently and effectively, without sacrificing the quality of your work.

So, my fellow jugglers, how do we balance all of these balls in the air at once? It's all about finding a rhythm and being adaptable. It's about knowing when to prioritize one ball over another, and when to shift your focus to a different one. With practice and perseverance, you too can become a master juggler of UX design in the real world.

User-First Design in a Real World: Addressing User Needs within Practical Constraints

As a UX designer, your role is not only about creating visually appealing and functional designs but also about understanding and addressing the needs of your users. However, in the real world, balancing user needs with other constraints, such as development limitations, business goals, and user adoption, requires collaboration with product managers and other stakeholders. In this chapter, we will explore how UX designers can work in tandem with stakeholders to identify and fulfill user needs in the most effective way.

> **User adoption** refers to the extent to which users successfully and willingly accept and integrate a product or service into their regular usage or behavior. It measures how well users are able to understand, learn, and utilize a product or service, and whether they find it valuable, enjoyable, and easy to use.
>
> **User adoption is a key metric for evaluating the success of a UX design**, as it indicates whether users are effectively engaging with and benefiting from the product or service. High user adoption rates typically indicate that the UX design has effectively met the needs and expectations of users, while low user adoption rates may suggest that the design needs improvements to better align with user requirements and preferences.

It's important to recognize that the responsibility of balancing user needs does not solely fall on the shoulders of UX designers. It requires collaboration with other stakeholders, including product managers, developers, and business owners, who provide valuable input based on their expertise and perspective. Collaborating with stakeholders can provide insights into business goals, technical limitations, and market trends that may impact the prioritization and implementation of user needs.

In addition to development limitations, user needs may also be constrained by other factors such as budget, timeline, and available resources. These constraints may limit the extent to which all user needs can be addressed comprehensively. In such cases, UX designers need to work closely with stakeholders to prioritize and make informed decisions about which user needs to prioritize and how to balance them with other constraints. Collaborative discussions, workshops, and brainstorming sessions can be effective in finding the right balance.

If I had asked people what they wanted, they would have said faster horses.

Henry Ford

> *This quote often attributed to Henry Ford, may not actually be his. While there is no evidence that Ford ever said these exact words, the sentiment behind the quote reflects his approach to innovation and his belief that it was the job of the innovator to anticipate and create solutions that people did not even know they needed yet.*

Users may not always be able to effectively communicate their needs or desires in a way that aligns with their actual requirements. This sentiment is captured in the famous quote (questionably) attributed to Henry Ford: "If I had asked people what they wanted, they would have said faster horses." Users may have a limited understanding of the potential solutions or may be influenced by their existing perceptions. As a UX designer, it is crucial to actively listen to user feedback but also to critically analyze and interpret it to uncover underlying needs that may not be explicitly stated. This requires careful consideration of the context, observation of user behavior, and empathetic understanding to identify the true pain points and opportunities for innovation. By going beyond surface-level feedback, a UX designer can create solutions that truly address user needs and result in a more meaningful and effective user experience.

To find what truly meets user needs, UX designers can leverage various research methods, such as user interviews, surveys, usability testing, and analytics, to gather insights and validate assumptions. Collaborating with stakeholders, including product managers and developers, can help in analyzing and interpreting user feedback and data to identify patterns and trends that can inform design decisions. This collaborative approach ensures that the final design solution is based on a holistic understanding of user needs and aligns with business goals and technical constraints.

Once the design solution is developed, it's important to effectively communicate and confirm that it meets the user's needs. UX designers can use various techniques, such as user testing, prototypes, and demos, to showcase the value and benefits of the design solution to users. Clear and concise communication that highlights how the design solution addresses their pain points and provides a positive user experience can help in gaining user buy-in and adoption.

Flexibility is crucial in the process of balancing user needs. UX designers need to be open to feedback, iterate on design solutions, and be willing to adapt based on changing user needs and project constraints. Collaborating with stakeholders, including product managers and developers, in an agile and iterative design process allows for continuous refinement of the design solution to better meet user needs.

Balancing user needs in UX design is a collaborative effort that involves working closely with stakeholders, including product managers, developers, and business owners. It requires careful consideration of development limitations, business goals, and user adoption, along with effective communication and interpretation of user feedback. By leveraging collaborative approaches, conducting research, and being flexible in the design process, UX designers can create solutions that effectively meet user needs and provide a positive user experience. And remember, sometimes users may not know what they really need, so don't be afraid to think outside the box and come up with the next "faster horse"!

UX Design on a Shoestring Budget - How to Create Awesome User Experiences with Limited Resources

As a UX designer, you're like a magician juggling limited resources - time, money, and manpower. It's like trying to pull a rabbit out of a hat with only a spoon and some tape. But fear not, my fellow design wizards! In this chapter, we'll explore how you can cast spells of creativity and innovation to create amazing user experiences, even when resources are scarce. And hey, maintaining a light-hearted approach can go a long way in preserving the magic of the process!

Time to Get Crafty: Prioritizing User Needs with a Wink and a Nod

When your budget resembles loose change you found in the couch cushions, and your timeline feels tighter than a pair of jeans after Thanksgiving dinner, it's time to get crafty. Prioritize user needs like a champ by identifying the most critical ones that align with your project goals and available resources. It's like playing a game of "Would You Rather" with your stakeholders — "Would you rather have a custom chatbot or a high-converting checkout process?" Embrace the challenge and make tough choices with a wink and a nod.

Abracadabra! Efficient Time Management to Keep the Magic Flowing

With limited resources, time becomes your most precious commodity. You'll need to work your time management magic to keep the project on track. Break down tasks into bite-sized chunks, and allocate your time wisely. Remember, you're not Hermione with a time-turner, so be realistic about what's achievable. And if you feel like you're running out of time, just shout "Accio more time!" (though no guarantees on its effectiveness).

Turning Lemons into Lemonade: Unleashing Creativity in the Face of Constraints

When resources are tight, it's time to don your creative hat and start brainstorming like a mad scientist. Turn those lemons into lemonade by finding innovative solutions within your constraints. Can't afford fancy custom illustrations? Embrace stock photos and add a clever twist with some witty captions. Short on manpower? Team up with other departments or enlist the help of office pets (if allowed). With a little creativity, you'll be amazed at what you can conjure up!

Hocus Pocus Usability Testing: Uncovering User Insights with a Hint of Magic

Usability testing doesn't have to be a formal, expensive affair. You can perform magic on a budget by conducting informal guerrilla testing or gathering feedback from a handful of users over a cup of coffee. Don't worry if your testing setup is more "MacGyver" than high-tech; it's the insights that count. And who knows, maybe a little magical charm will entice users to share their honest feedback with a twinkle in their eye.

Voila! Keeping Stakeholders in the Loop

When working with limited resources, communication is key to managing expectations and keeping everyone in the loop. But who says communication has to be dull? Add a dash of humor to your updates and progress reports to keep stakeholders engaged and entertained. Use gifs, memes, or even a classic dad joke to lighten the mood and maintain a magical rapport with your team and stakeholders.

Designing with limited resources can feel like performing magic tricks with a shoestring budget, but with creativity, and innovation you can create amazing user experiences that will leave your users spellbound. So, put on your wizard's hat, wave your UX wand, and let the magic of user-centered design unfold, even when resources are tight. After all, as Arthur C. Clarke said, "Any sufficiently advanced technology is indistinguishable from magic.

Taming the Tech Beast: Navigating Real-World Constraints with UX Wizardry

As a UX designer, you're not just dealing with the latest and greatest technology, but also the ever-changing landscape of the digital world. It's a beast that's constantly evolving, and sometimes it feels like you're in a wild rodeo, trying to stay on the saddle. But fear not, for you are the UX wizard who knows how to tame the tech beast with your wit and creativity!

Balancing Security and Usability: A High-Wire Act

One of the challenges you face in the real world is the delicate balancing act between security and usability. Stakeholders may demand airtight security measures, while users crave seamless and user-friendly experiences. It's like walking a tightrope, trying to find the sweet spot between robust security and delightful user experiences.

You've learned to work your magic by collaborating with security experts, developers, and other stakeholders to strike the right balance. You've navigated complex discussions with diplomacy, sometimes using analogies like comparing a security feature to a moat around a castle, but reminding everyone that the drawbridge should still be accessible to users without a secret code.

Managing User Expectations: The Reality Check

In the real world, users often have high expectations for technology, expect-ing it to solve all their problems and meet their every need. But you know that technology isn't always advanced enough to fulfill every user's wish. You've had to manage user expectations with a reality check, using your communication skills to gently explain that not every feature is feasible or practical.

You've become the "UX Realist," guiding stakeholders and users through the realm of technological possibilities and limitations. You've learned to prioritize features based on technical feasibility, user needs, and business goals, and you've used effective communication to soften the blow of saying "no" to unrealistic requests. You've even created a "Feature Wishlist" box where stakeholders can submit their wildest ideas, adding a touch of creativity to the process.

Embracing Change: The Only Constant in Technology

In the fast-paced world of technology, change is the only constant. New tools, frameworks, and languages are constantly emerging, and keeping up with the latest trends can sometimes feel like chasing a unicorn. But you've learned to embrace change with open arms.

You've become the "Tech Chameleon," adapting to new technologies and learning new skills with agility. You've embraced the mindset of lifelong learning, attending workshops, webinars, and meetups to stay up-to-date with the ever-evolving tech landscape. And when a new tool or framework comes out, you approach it with curiosity, like a kid in a candy store, ready to experiment and explore.

As we've explored, technology is constantly changing, resources can be limited, and constraints are an inevitable part of the real world of UX design. However, with your adaptability, creativity, and problem-solving skills, you are well-equipped to tame the tech beast and navigate these challenges with finesse. Remember to stay current with the latest tools and technologies, work collaboratively with developers, find workarounds when needed, and always keep the end user in mind. Embrace change, stay agile, and let your UX wizardry shine as you tackle real-world constraints and create exceptional user experiences.

Time Flies When You're UX Designing: Tackling Time Constraints with Finesse

As a savvy UX designer, you know that time is a hot commodity in the fast-paced world of design. Sure, you may have faced deadlines back in school, but the real deal of UX design comes with its own set of challenges when it comes to time constraints. Unlike school assignments with fixed requirements, the workplace can throw unexpected curveballs your way, with requirements shifting like a game of musical chairs, and deadlines stubbornly staying put. Navigating these time constraints requires you to be a time-wizard - agile, adaptive, and efficient - in your approach.

Juggling Evolving Requirements: In the real world of UX design, require-ments can change faster than a designer's mood board. Stakeholders may spring surprises, users' needs may take a U-turn, or market dynamics may do the cha-cha, and you need to be ready to roll with the punches. It's like playing a game of UX Tetris, fitting in the changes while still meeting the deadline. This calls for top-notch communication, collaboration, and prioritization skills to ensure that you deliver the best possible user experience within the given timeframe, even if the goalposts keep shifting.

Rolling with Last-Minute Updates: Unlike school assignments where requirements are etched in stone, the workplace can be a whirlwind of last-minute updates. From scope changes to shifting priorities to new insights from stakeholders, you may need to spin on a dime while keeping the original deadline in sight. It's like being a UX acrobat, making quick decisions, reprioritizing tasks, and redesigning elements on the fly to keep the project on track. Being flexible and adaptable in your approach is the name of the game to tackle these time constraints like a champ.

Jamming with Cross-Functional Teams: UX design projects often involve dancing with cross-functional teams, from developers to product managers to marketers, and more. Coordinating with different team members and aligning their efforts within the given timeframe can be a juggling act. It's like being the conductor of a UX orchestra, ensuring everyone is in sync and working towards the common goal of delivering a stellar user experience. Effective communication, timely feedback, and proactive collaboration are the moves that will keep you and your team grooving to the same beat.

Timing It Right in the Face of Uncertainty: Time constraints in UX design can sometimes be as unpredictable as the weather forecast. Project timelines may feel tighter than a pair of skinny jeans, and unexpected challenges may pop up like mushrooms after rain. It's like playing a UX game of whack-a-mole, where you need to manage your time like a pro. This may involve using time management techniques like prioritization, time blocking, and delegation to optimize your workflow and make every second count. Being proactive in identifying potential roadblocks and finding creative solutions is how you keep the clock on your side.

Keeping Your Cool and Staying Focused: Navigating time constraints in UX design can be like walking on a tightrope, but it's important to keep your balance. Don't let the pressure of deadlines and changing requirements send you into a design frenzy. Stay organized, communicate effectively, and prioritize tasks based on their impact and urgency. Remember to take breaks, and practice self-care to keep your sanity intact and your creativity flowing.

Remember to keep your cool, stay focused, and maintain a positive outlook to navigate the ups and downs of UX design in the real world. Embrace the unpredictable nature of the industry and find creative solutions to overcome constraints while keeping your sanity intact. With the right mindset, skills, and approach, you can thrive in the fast-paced world of UX design and create exceptional user experiences that delight users and stakeholders alike. So, put on your UX wizard hat, keep calm, and design on!

In the next chapter, we'll dive deeper into the art of communication —

another key skill for juggling multiple priorities and constraints. From collaborating with stakeholders to presenting your designs to clients, we'll explore how to communicate effectively and efficiently in the world of UX design. Stay tuned, my fellow jugglers!

* * *

Chapter 4: Talking to Non-Designers

Welcome to the world of UX design, where you're expected to be a mind reader and a magician all at once! In this chapter, we'll tackle one of the most challenging aspects of the job: communicating with non–designers.

From clueless stakeholders to picky clients, we'll explore the art of pretending you're on the same page as them. We'll share tips for translating design jargon into plain English, using visuals to illustrate your ideas, and navigating the minefield of feedback without losing your mind.

> The responses of members of the sub-species Non-Designer to their habitat can differ from those of humans in the other sub-species, Designer. The most frequently identified reason for these differences is that design training influences how humans experience the world around themselves.
>
> Sally Augustin, the founder of Design With Science

We'll also cover how to deal with the dreaded question, "Can you make it pop more?" and other requests that make you want to bang your head against the wall. Plus, we'll share stories of UX designers who had to resort to creative tactics like voodoo dolls and interpretive dance to get their ideas across.

By the end of this chapter, you'll be equipped with the skills to communicate like a pro and make sure everyone is on the same page (or at least in the same book). So grab your translator's hat and get ready to navigate the choppy waters of UX communication!

Lost in Translation: Navigating Communication in UX Design

Ahoy there, mateys! When it comes to UX design, communication is key. But navigating the treacherous waters of stakeholders and clients can be like navigating the Bermuda Triangle – full of surprises and potential pitfalls. Fear not, for we have some tips and tricks to help you stay afloat and reach the promised land of great UX!

Ahoy, Stakeholders!

First things first, when it comes to communicating with stakeholders and clients, it's important to speak their language. Using design jargon with them can be as confusing as trying to decipher ancient hieroglyphics. To avoid getting lost in translation, try to use everyday words and avoid technical terms unless necessary. And when you do need to use jargon, make sure to explain it in plain English. You don't want them feeling like they need a treasure map just to understand your design!

Show and Tell

Visual aids are like the X on the map that leads to buried treasure. Sketches, wireframes, and prototypes are your trusty sidekicks, helping to translate your design jargon into something everyone can understand. When presenting your designs, use visual aids to illustrate your ideas, and guide them through your thought process. This can help them understand the reasoning behind your design decisions, and can lead to more productive feedback. Just be prepared for some unexpected feedback. They might see a kraken where you see a mermaid.

Watch Your Step

Feedback can be as treacherous as the plank on a pirate ship. It's like walking through a minefield, with stakeholders and clients often having different opinions and priorities. To avoid getting blown out of the water, set expectations upfront. Explain your design process and what feedback you're looking for. This can help stakeholders and clients provide more productive feedback, and can help you avoid unnecessary revisions. But be prepared for some feedback that might make you feel like you're walking the plank. They might have some crazy ideas that you never considered, like a pirate ship with a hot tub.

Bridge Over Troubled Waters

Effective communication is like building a sturdy ship that can weather any storm. It's all about bridging the gap between designers and stake-holders/clients. One way to do this is to establish a shared vocabulary and understanding of design principles. This can help create a common language and expectations, leading to more effective communication. And don't forget to involve stakeholders and clients in the design process, creating a sense of ownership and investment in the final product. Who knows, they might have some amazing ideas that you never thought of, like a parrot that speaks UX jargon.

Communicating with stakeholders and clients is a critical aspect of UX design. In Chapter 9, we'll dive deeper into some of the specific issues that can arise when working with stakeholders and how to navigate them successfully. So, hoist the anchor, raise the sails, and let's set a course for great UX design!

Navigating Challenging Client Requests: From "Make it Pop" to Interpretive Dance

As a UX designer, you're going to come across clients who are picky, indecisive, and downright difficult to work with. They might ask you to make the button "pop" more, change the color scheme entirely, or add more features that are completely unnecessary. It's frustrating, to say the least, but it's part of the job.

First and foremost, it's important to remember that the client is paying you for a service. While it can be frustrating to make changes that you know are not in the best interest of the project, it's ultimately the client's decision. That being said, it's important to communicate the potential consequences of their requests. For example, if a client wants to add a feature that will significantly increase the development time, explain how it will impact the timeline and budget.

Another helpful tip is to use visuals to illustrate your ideas. If a client is having trouble understanding why a certain design element is necessary, create a visual mockup to show them how it works in context. This can help to bridge the gap between design jargon and plain English, making it easier for clients to understand your vision.

When dealing with picky clients, it's also important to keep your cool and stay professional. Don't let your frustration show, even if you feel like banging your head against the wall. Remember that you're there to provide a service, and maintaining a positive relationship with the client is key to ensuring a successful project.

Here are some stories from the field of UX design:

- **The Comic Strip Presentation:** A UX designer was tasked with presenting a complex user flow to a cross-functional team. Instead of using traditional slides, the designer decided to create a comic strip-style presentation. Using simple illustrations and speech bubbles, the designer crafted a visual story that walked the team through each step of the user flow. The comic strip presentation was engaging, visually appealing, and helped the team grasp the user experience in a more intuitive way.
- **The Metaphor Metamorphosis:** During a design review, a UX designer found it challenging to explain the abstract concept of information architecture to non-designers. To make it more relatable, the designer came up with a metaphor comparing information architecture to the layout of a grocery store. The designer explained how categories, subcategories, and navigation pathways in a website are similar to the layout of different sections in a grocery store, making it easier for stakeholders to understand and provide feedback on the design.
- **The User Journey Map:** In a brainstorming session, a UX designer wanted to convey the pain points and opportunities of a user's experience with a digital product. Instead of using bullet points or slides, the designer created a visual user journey map. Using sticky notes and a whiteboard, the designer mapped out the user's journey from discovery to onboarding

to regular usage, highlighting pain points and opportunities at each stage. The user journey map provided a holistic view of the user's experience and facilitated a meaningful discussion among the team.

- **The Prototyping Playtime:** In a usability testing session, a UX designer was struggling to gather feedback from users who were hesitant to provide criticism. To encourage open feedback, the designer decided to turn the session into a "prototyping playtime." The designer created a low-fidelity prototype using paper and markers and invited users to play with it, experiment, and provide feedback in a playful and non-threatening environment. The users were more comfortable providing candid feedback, leading to valuable insights for improving the design.

In the end, effective communication in UX design requires a combination of skills and strategies. By learning how to speak the language of your stakeholders, using visuals to communicate your ideas, and navigating feedback with confidence, you can successfully translate your vision into reality. And who knows, maybe one day you'll even find yourself reaching for that voodoo doll.

So, what can you do to deal with these frustrating requests and still maintain a good working relationship with your client? Here are a few tips:

- **Clarify the request:** When a client makes a vague or ambiguous request, it's important to clarify exactly what they mean. Ask them to explain in more detail or provide specific examples of what they are looking for.
- **Focus on the problem:** Instead of getting hung up on the request itself, try to identify the underlying problem the client is trying to solve. This can help you come up with more effective solutions that address their needs while still staying true to the design.
- **Educate the client:** Many clients may not be familiar with the design process or the technical aspects of UX design. Take the time to explain the reasoning behind your design decisions and the limitations of what can

be achieved. This can help them better understand why certain requests may not be possible or practical.

- **Stay flexible:** Sometimes, even with the best of intentions, a client may request changes that are simply not feasible. In these cases, it's important to stay flexible and open to alternative solutions. Work with the client to identify other options that may achieve the same goals while still staying true to the design.

Remember, dealing with difficult clients is a part of the job, but it doesn't have to be a nightmare. By staying calm, professional, and solution-focused, you can build stronger relationships with your clients and create designs that meet their needs while still staying true to your own vision.

The Great Dev Debate: Navigating Communication in UX Design with Developers

Communicating with developers can be a tricky business, much like trying to teach a goldfish to do a backflip. They have their own language and priorities, and it can be challenging to get them on board with your design vision. Fear not, brave designer, for in this chapter, we'll explore some tips and tricks to navigate the communication minefield and ensure you and your developers are on the same page.

Speak Their Code and Make Code Your King

Designers and developers may speak different languages, with acronyms, abbreviations, and jargon that can be overwhelming. To bridge this gap, it's important to learn some basic coding language and use it to communicate your design ideas effectively. Understand their technical limitations and explain your designs in terms of code to gain their appreciation. However, avoid attempting to code your designs unless you're proficient, as it may result in a messy outcome like a spaghetti monster.

Developers are passionate about code and its endless possibilities, like a pirate with their treasure. To ensure alignment with your design vision, demonstrate how your designs can be coded. Familiarize yourself with HTML, CSS, and JavaScript, even at a basic level, to create designs that are feasible to implement and won't break the website. If coding isn't your forte, collaborate with developers and find a compromise, like a frog and a fish working together in a pond.

Did you just mention spaghetti monster? What is it?

Imagine you have a big bowl of spaghetti with lots of tangled noodles that are all mixed up and hard to follow. That's what **"spaghetti code"** means in computer programming. **It's a messy and disorganized way of writing code** where different parts of a computer program are intertwined and hard to understand. Just like how it's challenging to untangle a bowl of spaghetti, spaghetti code can make it difficult for programmers to fix or update a program because it's confusing and chaotic. It's important for programmers to write clean and organized code, so it's easy to understand and maintain in the future.

Illustrate Your Design Vision

Visual aids aren't just for stakeholders and clients – they're also incredibly helpful when communicating with developers. They're like a superhero cape that makes your designs come to life. Use sketches, wireframes, and prototypes to illustrate your design ideas and show developers how they should function. This can help them understand the user experience you're aiming for and can lead to more productive feedback. Just don't be surprised if they ask you to explain your design in terms of a mathematical formula. They like to keep things logical, unlike a unicorn with its magical rainbow powers.

Bridge the Gap

At the end of the day, effective communication between designers and developers is all about bridging the gap between the creative and technical worlds. One way to bridge this gap is to involve developers in the design process from the beginning, creating a sense of ownership and investment in the final product. This can also help you understand their technical limitations and find solutions that work for everyone. Just be prepared for some friendly debates. You might think your design is as perfect as a unicorn, but they might see some technical issues you never considered, like a dragon with an itch they can't scratch.

Communicating with developers can be challenging, but it's essential to create great user experiences. By speaking their code, visualizing your vision, respecting their coding skills, and bridging the gap, you can overcome communication barriers and create products that both look good and function well. So let's raise a glass to good communication and great UX design, like a mermaid riding a narwhal through a sea of creative collaboration!

* * *

Chapter 5: UX Pitfalls - A Beginner's Guide to Failing

Developing exceptional user experiences is a multifaceted task that demands attention to detail, innovative problem-solving, and an unwavering focus on user needs. As UX designers, we are tasked with creating designs that are not only easy to use and intuitive but also solve real-world problems for our users. Despite our best intentions, things don't always go as planned, and we are faced with the occasional UX failure. However, these failures can provide valuable lessons for future design iterations.

In this chapter, we will take a deep dive into some common UX pitfalls that you may encounter and explore how to turn these failures into opportunities for growth. By embracing the mistakes we make as UX designers, we can learn from them, iterate on our designs, and ultimately create better experiences for our users.

The first pitfall is **assuming** that you know what users want. Why bother doing user research when you can just assume what users need? After all, you're the designer, and you know best! Forget about gathering feedback throughout the design process - just make sure to rely on your own assumptions, and watch as your designs flop.

The second pitfall is **designing for the "average" user**. Who cares about designing for specific user groups when you can just design for the mythical "average" user? By designing for the average, you can totally exclude certain segments of your user base and alienate them. Why design for inclusivity when you can just design for the majority?

The third pitfall is **neglecting accessibility**. Accessibility is overrated, and it's not like you need to create designs that are usable by everyone, regardless of their abilities. Just forget about accessibility, and make your designs exclusive to certain user groups. That'll show 'em who's boss!

The fourth pitfall is **designing for aesthetics over functionality**. Who needs functionality when you can have a pretty design? Functionality is boring, and it's not like users need to be able to actually use your design effectively. Just focus on making things look pretty, and you'll have a surefire way to fail.

And finally, the fifth pitfall is **neglecting the importance of testing**. Why bother testing your designs when you can just assume they're perfect? Testing is overrated, and it's not like you need to gather feedback from real users to ensure that your designs are meeting their needs. Just launch your designs without any testing, and watch as they crash and burn.

Embracing these common UX pitfalls is key to failing miserably. By prioritizing your assumptions, designing for the mythical "average" user, neglecting accessibility, focusing on aesthetics over functionality, and skipping testing altogether, you can create designs that are ineffective, confusing, and exclusive. In the next chapter, we'll explore how to design for different platforms and devices, but let's be real, you'll probably just mess that up too. Good luck!

The Pitfall of Assumptions: Navigating the Dangers of Making Assumptions in UX Design

As a UX designer, you strive to create designs that meet the needs and expectations of your users. However, one common pitfall that can hinder the success of your UX projects is making assumptions. Assumptions are beliefs or judgments that we hold without verifying them, and they can lead to inaccurate or incomplete understanding of users, their behaviors, and their needs. Navigating the dangers of making assumptions is crucial to ensure that your designs are effective, user-centered, and aligned with the goals of your project.

The Perils of Unverified Assumptions: When you make assumptions about your users or their needs, you are at risk of creating designs that may not meet their expectations. Unverified assumptions can result in misleading or incomplete insights, leading to designs that do not address the real needs of users. For example, assuming that all users have the same level of technical proficiency or that they prefer a particular design style without proper research can result in designs that are difficult to use or fail to resonate with the target audience.

The Impact on User Experience: Assumptions can have a direct impact on the overall user experience of your designs. If your assumptions about user behavior or preferences are incorrect, it can result in confusing or frustrating experiences for users. Users may struggle to complete tasks, find information, or achieve their goals, leading to poor usability, low engagement, and even user abandonment. The negative impact on user experience can have serious consequences, such as loss of customers, negative reviews, and damage to the reputation of your product or brand.

The Role of User Research: User research is a critical component of UX design that helps you uncover the real needs, behaviors, and preferences of your users. It involves methods such as interviews, surveys, observations, and usability testing to collect data and insights that inform your design decisions. By conducting user research, you can validate or invalidate assumptions, gain a deeper understanding of your users, and create designs that are based on solid evidence rather than subjective beliefs.

Challenges in User Research: Conducting user research can come with its own set of challenges. It requires time, effort, and resources to plan, execute, and analyze research activities. There may be limitations in terms of budget, timeline, or access to users. Additionally, interpreting research findings and translating them into design decisions can be complex, as research results may be open to interpretation and require careful analysis. However, the benefits of user research far outweigh the challenges, as it helps you make informed design decisions and reduces the risks of making assumptions.

To avoid the pitfalls of assumptions in UX design, it's important to adopt strategies that promote evidence-based decision-making. Here are some strategies to consider:

- **Conduct User Research:** Invest time and effort in conducting user research to gather data and insights about your users. Use a variety of research methods to collect qualitative and quantitative data that can inform your design decisions.
- **Validate Assumptions:** Whenever possible, validate your assumptions with real data from user research. Test your assumptions through usability testing, interviews, or surveys to ensure that they align with the actual behaviors and preferences of your users.
- **Seek User Feedback:** Involve users in the design process and seek their feedback at different stages of the project. Get their input on early design concepts, prototypes, and final designs to ensure that your assumptions are on track and that the design meets their needs.
- **Collaborate with Stakeholders:** Collaborate with stakeholders, including product managers, developers, and other team members, to gather their insights and perspectives. Avoid assumptions about their requirements or constraints and actively seek their input to ensure that your designs align with their expectations.
- **Embrace Iterative Design:** Embrace an iterative design process that allows for continuous testing, learning, and refinement. Avoid making assumptions about the success of your design without validating it through user feedback and data analysis. Iterate on your designs based on the insights gained from user research and feedback to continually improve the user experience.
- **Consider Diversity:** Avoid assuming that all users are the same or have similar needs and preferences. Consider the diversity among your user base, including factors such as age, gender, culture, abilities, and context of use. Design inclusively, taking into account the needs of different user segments, to ensure that your designs are accessible, inclusive, and relevant to a wider audience.
- **Keep an Open Mind:** Be open to challenging your own assumptions and be willing to revise your designs based on new insights. Avoid being rigid

in your assumptions and remain open to feedback, critique, and new perspectives. Embrace a growth mindset that encourages continuous learning and improvement.

· **Test Early and Often:** Testing your designs early and often with real users can help you validate or invalidate assumptions and identify any usability issues or pain points. Conduct usability testing, A/B testing, or other forms of testing to gather data that can inform your design decisions and ensure that your assumptions are aligned with user behavior.

A user interface is like a joke. If you have to explain it, it's not that good.

Martin LeBlanc, the CEO and founder of IconFinder

Avoiding assumptions is a crucial aspect of UX design to ensure that your designs are effective, user-centered, and aligned with the needs and preferences of your users. By conducting user research, seeking user feedback, collaborating with stakeholders, embracing an iterative design process, considering diversity, keeping an open mind, and testing early and often, you can navigate the dangers of assumptions and create exceptional user experiences that meet the needs and expectations of your users. So, keep your assumptions in check, and let data and user insights be your guiding light in creating delightful user experiences! Happy designing!

The Perils of Designing for the "Average" User

As a UX designer, it's easy to fall into the trap of designing for the mythical "average" user. After all, it seems like a convenient way to streamline your design process and cater to the majority. However, designing for the average user can be a significant pitfall that leads to the exclusion and alienation of specific user groups.

Excluding User Diversity: Designing for the average user often ignores the reality that users come from diverse backgrounds, with different abilities, preferences, and needs. By designing for the average, you risk neglecting the unique requirements of specific user segments, such as users with disabilities, users from different cultural backgrounds, or users with different age groups. This can result in excluding these users from fully accessing and enjoying your product or service, leading to a subpar user experience.

Recognize and embrace the diversity among your user base. Conduct user research to understand the unique needs, preferences, and abilities of different user segments. Consider factors such as age, culture, gender, and abilities in your design process.

Ignoring Edge Cases: The average user is just that — an average. But what about the outliers, the edge cases, and the uncommon scenarios? These users may have different needs or use cases that deviate from the norm. By focusing solely on the average, you may miss out on addressing these unique use cases, resulting in usability issues or frustration for these users.

Don't ignore the outliers and edge cases. Consider scenarios that deviate from the norm and design for them to ensure a seamless experience for all users, including those with unique use cases.

Lack of Personalization: Users expect personalized experiences that cater to their individual needs and preferences. Designing for the average user may not provide the level of personalization that users desire, leading to a generic and impersonal experience. In today's competitive landscape, personalization is becoming a key differentiator, and failing to account for it in your design can lead to missed opportunities and decreased user satisfaction.

Explore opportunities to personalize the user experience based on individual user preferences, behaviors, and context of use. This can help create a more engaging and relevant experience for users, leading to increased satisfaction and loyalty.

Missed Business Opportunities: By only designing for the average user, you may overlook potential business opportunities in catering to specific user segments. Understanding and addressing the unique needs of different user groups can open up new markets, increase user engagement, and drive customer loyalty. Ignoring these opportunities can result in lost revenue and market share.

Look beyond the average user and identify potential business opportunities in catering to specific user segments. Conduct market research and user analysis to uncover untapped markets and user needs that align with your business objectives.

Ethical Considerations: Designing exclusively for the average user can raise ethical concerns, particularly in areas such as inclusivity and diversity. It's important to consider the ethical implications of your design decisions and ensure that your design is inclusive, accessible, and respectful of diverse user groups. Ignoring these ethical considerations can lead to reputational damage and legal issues.

Consider the ethical implications of your design decisions and ensure that your design promotes inclusivity, diversity, and respect for all users. Be mindful of potential biases and discriminatory practices in your design, and strive to create an ethical user experience that aligns with your values and principles.

Designing for the average user can be a significant pitfall in UX design. It can lead to exclusion, lack of personalization, missed business opportunities, and ethical concerns. By avoiding the trap of designing for the average and instead designing for the diverse needs and preferences of your entire user base, you can create user experiences that are inclusive, engaging, and impactful, resulting in happy and satisfied users. So, remember, don't settle for the average, strive for exceptional user experiences that delight all users!

The Pitfall of Neglecting Accessibility: Why Inclusive Design Matters

As a UX designer, you may have come across the misconception that accessibility is overrated or not necessary in the design process. However, neglecting accessibility can be a significant pitfall that can have detrimental consequences for your users and your design outcomes. In this chapter, we'll explore why inclusive design, which encompasses accessibility, is crucial for creating user experiences that are truly inclusive, usable, and ethical.

The Myth of Accessibility being Overrated: Accessibility is not just a buzzword, but a fundamental aspect of UX design. It's about creating designs that are usable by everyone, regardless of their abilities, disabilities, or impairments. Neglecting accessibility means excluding users with disabilities, limiting their access to information, services, and products, and perpetuating discrimination and inequality. Accessibility is not overrated; it's a basic human right, and as UX designers, we have a responsibility to ensure that our designs are inclusive and accessible to all users, regardless of their abilities.

Excluding User Groups: Neglecting accessibility in your design can result in excluding certain user groups from accessing and using your product or service. This can include users with visual impairments, hearing impairments, motor disabilities, cognitive disabilities, and other disabilities. By ignoring accessibility, you are limiting the opportunities for these users to engage with your design, resulting in a negative user experience and potential legal and ethical implications. Neglecting accessibility is not only discriminatory but also a missed opportunity to cater to a diverse user base and expand your reach.

Ethical Concerns: Neglecting accessibility can raise ethical concerns in UX design. It goes against the principles of inclusivity, fairness, and equality. It's important to consider the ethical implications of excluding certain user groups and perpetuating discrimination through design. As UX designers, we have a responsibility to ensure that our designs do not discriminate against users with disabilities and that they are provided with equal access to information, services, and products. Ethical considerations should be at the forefront of our design decisions, and neglecting accessibility can have severe ethical repercussions.

Legal and Business Implications: Neglecting accessibility can also have legal and business implications. Many countries have laws and regulations that mandate accessibility in digital products and services, and non-compliance can result in legal action, fines, and damage to the brand's reputation. Moreover, neglecting accessibility can limit your business opportunities, as you may be excluding potential customers who have disabilities or impairments. By neglecting accessibility, you are not only risking legal and financial consequences but also missing out on a significant market segment.

The Importance of Inclusive Design: Inclusive design, which encompasses accessibility, is crucial for creating user experiences that are truly inclusive, usable, and ethical. It involves considering the diverse needs, preferences, and abilities of all users and designing with empathy and inclusivity in mind. Inclusive design focuses on removing barriers, providing alternatives, and creating user experiences that are flexible, adaptable, and inclusive to all users, regardless of their abilities or disabilities. By embracing inclusive design, you are not only creating user experiences that are accessible to everyone but also fostering a culture of inclusivity, empathy, and ethical design practices.

Neglecting accessibility is a significant pitfall in UX design that can have negative consequences for users, businesses, and ethical considerations. Embracing inclusive design, which encompasses accessibility, is crucial for creating user experiences that are truly inclusive, usable, and ethical. As UX designers, it's our responsibility to ensure that our designs are accessible to all users, regardless of their abilities, disabilities, or impairments. By prioritizing accessibility and embracing inclusive design principles, we can create impactful and inclusive user experiences that make a positive difference in the lives of all users. Let's strive to design with empathy, inclusivity, and accessibility in mind, and create user experiences that leave no one behind.

Falling for Aesthetic Overload

The fourth pitfall in UX design is prioritizing aesthetics over functionality. Who needs a functional design when you can have something that looks pretty, right? After all, functionality is just boring and overrated. Who cares if users can actually use your design effectively? Just make it look nice, and you'll be guaranteed to fail!

But, hold on a second. While aesthetics are certainly important in UX design, they should never take precedence over functionality. A visually appealing design is great, but if it doesn't serve the needs of the users or fulfill the goals of the design, then it's simply eye candy without substance. The primary purpose of UX design is to create experiences that are usable, efficient, and effective for users. Aesthetics should always be considered in the context of how they contribute to the overall functionality and usability of the design.

Designing for aesthetics over functionality can lead to a host of problems. Users may struggle to understand how to use the design, or they may encounter obstacles in achieving their goals. This can result in frustration, poor user satisfaction, and ultimately, abandonment of the design. A pretty design that lacks functionality is like a sports car with no engine - it may look flashy, but it won't get you anywhere.

To avoid falling into the pitfall of designing for aesthetics over functionality, UX designers should always prioritize usability and functionality in their design decisions. This includes conducting thorough user research, understanding user needs and goals, creating intuitive navigation and interaction patterns, and conducting thorough usability testing to ensure that the design meets the needs of the users effectively. It's also important to collaborate closely with other stakeholders, such as developers and product managers, to ensure that the design is not compromised for the sake of aesthetics alone.

While aesthetics are undoubtedly important in UX design, they should never take precedence over functionality. A visually appealing design should always be paired with usability, efficiency, and effectiveness to create meaningful and impactful user experiences. As UX designers, it's crucial to strike a balance between aesthetics and functionality, ensuring that our designs are not just visually pleasing, but also user-friendly and purposeful. So, let's resist the temptation of prioritizing aesthetics over functionality and create designs that not only look good but also work great!

Ignoring the Power of Testing

The fifth pitfall in UX design is neglecting the importance of testing. Who needs to test their designs when you can just assume they're perfect, right? Testing is overrated, and gathering feedback from real users to ensure that your designs are meeting their needs is just a waste of time. Just launch your designs without any testing and watch them crash and burn. Easy peasy, right?

Well, not so fast. Testing is a critical aspect of UX design that should never be overlooked. Assuming that your designs are perfect without validating them with real users can lead to disastrous consequences. Users are diverse, and their needs, preferences, and behaviors can vary greatly. What may seem intuitive and straightforward to you as a designer may not be the same for your users. Testing is the key to identifying usability issues, uncovering pain points, and gathering valuable feedback that can inform design improvements.

Neglecting testing can result in a design that fails to meet user expectations, frustrates users, and leads to low user satisfaction. It can also result in wasted resources, time, and effort in developing a design that ultimately does not resonate with the target audience. Just like you wouldn't launch a rocket without rigorous testing, you shouldn't launch a design without putting it to the test with real users.

UX designers should incorporate various testing methods into their design process, such as usability testing, A/B testing, focus groups, and feedback sessions with real users. These testing methods can provide invaluable insights into how users interact with the design, what works, what doesn't, and what improvements can be made. Testing should be an ongoing process throughout the design lifecycle, from initial prototypes to final products, to ensure continuous improvement and optimization.

Testing is a crucial aspect of UX design that should never be neglected. So, let's embrace the power of testing and use it as a valuable tool to create user-centric designs that truly resonate with our target audience.

* * *

Chapter 6: Navigating the Maze of Device Diversity

D esigning for different platforms is like navigating a maze, but with the right approach, you can create a seamless user experience that shines on all devices. Whether it's a desktop, a mobile device, or a wearable, responsive and adaptive design are the superpowers that ensure your users can access your content and services with ease.

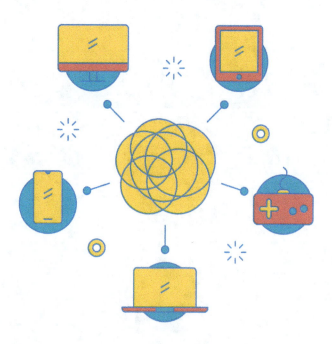

Gone are the days of static design that only caters to a single device. **Responsive design** is like a chameleon that adapts to its surroundings, ensuring your website or app looks and performs optimally on any screen size. It's like having a magic wand that transforms your design into a user-friendly masterpiece, regardless of whether it's viewed on a big desktop monitor or a tiny smartphone screen.

But responsive design alone may not be enough. Enter **adaptive design**, the sidekick that takes user experience to the next level. Adaptive design goes beyond just resizing elements, it considers the unique characteristics of each device and tailors the experience accordingly. It's like having a wardrobe of custom-tailored suits for different occasions - your design should look and feel natural on each device, providing a seamless experience that feels native to the platform.

Creating a desktop design that requires users to pinch, zoom, and scroll endlessly is like trying to juggle flaming torches while riding a unicycle. It's a recipe for disaster! Instead, prioritize a clean layout, easy navigation, and meaningful interactions that delight users on desktop devices. Don't make them work for it, make it effortless for them to find what they need and achieve their goals.

When it comes to **mobile design**, it's not just about squeezing your desktop design into a smaller screen. It's about understanding the unique characteristics of mobile devices, such as touch-based interactions and on-the-go usage, and optimizing your design accordingly. Think of it as designing for a fast-paced game of tag - users should be able to tap, swipe, and scroll with ease, without getting caught up in a web of tiny buttons and links.

Designing for **wearables** is like solving a puzzle with ever-changing pieces. These tiny devices require a whole new level of creativity and innovation. Users interact with wearables in a glanceable manner, expecting quick and relevant information at a glance. It's like designing a magic trick - you need to surprise and delight users with just the right amount of information, revealed at the right moment.

So, buckle up and get ready to navigate the maze of device diversity as we unlock the secrets to a seamless user experience with responsive and adaptive design. Whether you're a web designer, app developer, or UX enthusiast, this chapter will provide you with the insights you need to create exceptional user experiences across all devices. Let's dive in and discover how responsive and adaptive design can transform your digital creations into true superheroes of UX!

Responsive Design vs Adaptive Design: Unleashing the Battle of Web Design Titans!

Once upon a time, in the mystical realm of web design, there were two titans that battled for supremacy – Responsive Design and Adaptive Design. Both had their unique strengths and abilities, and webmasters around the world were torn between them, unable to decide which one was the ultimate victor. So, let's dive into the epic showdown of Responsive Design vs Adaptive Design and see which one comes out on top!

Round 1: Flexibility

Responsive Design: With its flexible layout, responsive design is like a shape-shifter, adapting to different screen sizes with ease. It uses CSS media queries to adjust the layout, ensuring that the website looks good on any device, from desktops to tablets to smartphones. It's a one-size-fits-all approach that offers consistency across all devices.

Adaptive Design: Adaptive design, on the other hand, is like a chameleon, changing its appearance based on the device. It delivers different versions of the same page, each designed specifically for a particular device. It gives webmasters more control over the user experience on different screens, allowing for customization.

Winner: It's a tie! Both responsive and adaptive design offer flexibility, but in different ways. Responsive design provides a consistent experience across all devices, while adaptive design allows for more customization. It's a matter of personal preference and specific project requirements.

Round 2: Development Complexity

Responsive Design: Responsive design requires a single layout to be designed and developed, using CSS media queries to adjust the layout based on screen size. It's a simpler approach, as there's only one codebase to maintain, and changes can be made universally.

Adaptive Design: Adaptive design, on the other hand, requires multiple versions of the same page to be designed and developed, each tailored for a specific device. It's more complex, as there are multiple codebases to maintain, and changes need to be made separately for each version.

Winner: Responsive Design! In terms of development complexity, responsive design takes the lead as it requires a single codebase to maintain, making it more efficient and cost-effective in the long run.

Round 3: User Experience

Responsive Design: Responsive design offers a consistent user experience across all devices, as the layout adjusts seamlessly to fit the screen size. It ensures that the website is accessible and usable on any device, providing a smooth and cohesive user journey.

Adaptive Design: Adaptive design, with its customized layouts for different devices, allows for more control over the user experience. Each version of the page can be optimized for the specific capabilities and constraints of the device, providing a tailored experience.

Winner: Adaptive Design! When it comes to user experience, adaptive design takes the lead as it allows for more customization, ensuring that the website provides an optimized experience on each device.

Round 4: Future-proofing

Responsive Design: Responsive design is future-proof to some extent, as it can adapt to different screen sizes, including those of devices that don't exist yet. It's a forward-thinking approach that ensures the website remains accessible on future devices.

Adaptive Design: Adaptive design, on the other hand, requires separate versions of the page for each device, which may not be compatible with future devices. It may require additional development and maintenance efforts to keep up with new devices and screen sizes.

Winner: Responsive Design! In terms of future-proofing, responsive design takes the lead as it provides more flexibility to adapt to future devices without the need for major changes.

Final Verdict: It's a Draw!

The battle between **Responsive Design** and **Adaptive Design** ends in a **draw**! Both approaches have their strengths and weaknesses, and the ultimate winner depends on the specific needs and goals of the web project. Responsive design offers simplicity, consistency, and cost-effectiveness, making it a great choice for projects that require a unified user experience across different devices. On the other hand, adaptive design provides more customization and control over the user experience, making it suitable for projects that demand tailored experiences on different devices.

But hey, why choose just one? Just like peanut butter and jelly, responsive design and adaptive design can be a perfect combination! You can use a combination of both approaches to create a hybrid solution that best meets your project's needs. For example, you can use responsive design as a baseline for a consistent layout across devices, and then add adaptive design elements to further optimize the user experience on specific devices or screen sizes.

So, whether you choose to go with the shape-shifting powers of responsive design or the chameleon-like abilities of adaptive design, the key is to understand the strengths and limitations of each approach and make an informed decision based on your project's unique requirements. Happy designing, and may the web design titans continue their battle for eternity, creating amazing web experiences for users around the world! And remember, the most important tip of all: always have fun and let your creativity soar as you design the web of tomorrow!

Designing for the Big Screen: Creating Engaging Experiences for Large Displays

In today's digital world, large screens are becoming more prevalent than ever. From massive video walls in stadiums to expansive displays in corporate lobbies, airports, and hospitals, large screens offer unique design opportunities to create visually stunning and engaging experiences. Let's dive into the world of designing for large screens and explore some tips and examples for creating impactful designs.

Embrace the Canvas: Think Big, Think Bold

When designing for large screens, you have a vast canvas to work with, and it's essential to embrace it fully. Think big, think bold! Large screens provide ample space to showcase your content, whether it's data visualizations, videos, images, or interactive elements. Utilize the full-screen real estate to create a visually compelling experience that captures the attention of your audience.

For example, in a hospital dashboard displayed on a large monitor, you can use the screen space to display critical patient information, real-time data, and analytics in a visually appealing and easy-to-understand format. You can use large fonts, vivid colors, and clear visuals to make the information easily accessible and actionable for healthcare professionals.

Simplify and Focus: Less is More

When designing for large screens, it's crucial to simplify your content and focus on the most critical information or message you want to convey. Avoid cluttering the screen with too much content or unnecessary elements that can overwhelm the viewer. Remember, less is more!

Consider the viewing distance and angle of the large screen and ensure that the content is easily readable and accessible from a distance. Use clear typography, contrasting colors, and simple visual elements that are easy to understand and interpret, even from a distance.

For instance, in a corporate lobby display showcasing company achievements and milestones, you can use minimalistic design elements such as large, bold typography, clean icons, and simple graphics to convey the key messages clearly and concisely.

Leverage Interactivity: Engage and Involve

One of the unique advantages of designing for large screens is the opportunity to incorporate interactivity into your designs. Interactivity can enhance user engagement and create memorable experiences.

Consider incorporating touch or gesture-based interactions, if applicable, to allow users to interact with the content on the large screen. This can be especially effective in interactive installations, exhibits, or wayfinding displays, where users can actively engage with the content and explore information or options.

For example, in an airport information kiosk with a large screen, users can interact with the display to access flight information, maps, and other

REAL UX: PRACTICAL GUIDE

relevant details, creating an engaging and informative experience.

Consider the Context: Design for the Environment

When designing for large screens, it's crucial to consider the environment where the display will be installed. Factors such as lighting conditions, viewing distance, and viewing angle can significantly impact the effectiveness of your design.

For example, in a brightly lit airport terminal with high levels of ambient light, you may need to use high contrast colors, bold typography, and large visuals to ensure that the content is easily visible and readable. Similarly, if the display is installed in a public space with multiple viewing angles, you may need to consider the visibility from different perspectives and adjust your design accordingly.

Designing for large screens requires thorough testing and optimization to ensure that the content is visually appealing, accessible, and effective in conveying the intended message. Test your designs on the actual large screen to see how they look and perform in the real environment.

Pay attention to details such as font sizes, color contrasts, and readability from different viewing distances. Fine-tune your designs based on feedback and real-world testing to ensure that they deliver the desired impact.

Examples of Large Screen Designs

Airport Flight Information Display System

Large screens are commonly used in airports to display real-time flight information for travelers. These displays typically show flight numbers, departure and arrival times, gate numbers, and status updates, allowing passengers to quickly and easily access the information they need to navigate their travel plans.

- **Dynamic Animations:** Use subtle animations to draw attention to important information, such as flight status updates or gate changes. Animations can provide visual cues that catch the users' attention and make the information more engaging.

- **Multi-language Support:** Consider adding support for multiple languages to cater to the diverse group of travelers in airports. This can include displaying flight information in different languages or providing language selection options to accommodate international travelers.
- **Emergency Alerts:** Incorporate a system for displaying emergency alerts, such as weather advisories, security announcements, or evacuation instructions, to ensure the safety of travelers in case of emergencies.

Command and Control Centers

Large screens are often used in command and control centers, such as those in military operations or emergency response centers, to provide a comprehensive overview of critical information. These displays can show maps, live video feeds, data visualizations, and other relevant information to help decision-makers monitor and manage complex situations in real-time.

- **Customizable Layouts:** Allow users to customize the layout of the large screen display based on their specific needs and preferences. This can include rearranging or resizing different information panels or data visualizations to suit the users' workflow and priorities.
- **Real-time Notifications:** Implement a notification system that alerts users to critical events or updates in real-time. This can include visual or audible notifications for important alarms, alerts, or messages to ensure that decision-makers are promptly informed of any changes or incidents.
- **Interactive Maps:** Incorporate interactive maps with real-time data overlays, such as GPS tracking of assets, personnel, or vehicles, to provide comprehensive situational awareness and aid in decision-making.

Concert or Event Displays

Large screens are frequently used in concerts, sports events, and other large-scale gatherings to provide a visual experience for the audience. These displays can show live video feeds, close-up shots of performers, and other visual elements that enhance the overall event experience for the attendees.

- **Immersive Visuals:** Use high-quality, high-resolution visuals that enhance the overall event experience for the audience. This can include live video feeds, close-up shots of performers, and visually appealing graphics that align with the event's theme or branding.
- **Social Media Integration:** Integrate social media feeds or interactive features that allow event attendees to engage with the event and share their experiences on social media platforms, creating a buzz and promoting the event online.
- **Live Polling or Voting:** Incorporate interactive elements that allow event attendees to participate in live polls, voting, or surveys to encourage engagement and gather valuable feedback.

Digital Signage

Large screens are widely used in digital signage applications, such as in shopping malls, airports, or transportation hubs, to display advertisements, announcements, or other relevant information to a large audience. These displays can be interactive, allowing users to interact with the content or provide feedback.

- **Content Scheduling:** Implement a scheduling system that allows content to be updated and scheduled to display at specific times or dates. This can ensure that relevant and timely information is displayed to the intended audience at the right time.
- **Interactive Touchscreen:** Incorporate interactive touchscreen capabilities that allow users to interact with the content, such as selecting

options, browsing through products, or providing feedback. This can create a more engaging and personalized experience for users.

- **Content Management System:** Provide an easy-to-use content management system that allows content to be updated and managed remotely. This can enable quick and efficient content updates, ensuring that the displayed information is always up-to-date and relevant.

Museum Exhibits

Large screens are commonly used in museums to provide interactive exhibits or educational displays. These displays can show multimedia content, interactive maps, or simulations, allowing visitors to engage with the information in a visually appealing and immersive way.

- **Multi-modal Interactivity:** Incorporate different modalities of interaction, such as touchscreens, gesture recognition, or voice commands, to cater to different user preferences and accessibility needs. This can provide a more inclusive and engaging experience for all museum visitors.
- **Gamification Elements:** Include gamification elements, such as quizzes, challenges, or rewards, to make the exhibits more interactive and enjoyable for visitors. This can encourage active participation and enhance the educational experience.
- **Contextual Information:** Provide contextual information and visual cues that help visitors understand the relevance and significance of the exhibits. This can include maps, timelines, or multimedia content that provide additional context and enrich the overall learning experience.

Data Visualization Dashboards

Large screens are often used in businesses or organizations to display real-time data visualization dashboards for monitoring key metrics, such as sales data, production statistics, or social media analytics. These displays can

REAL UX: PRACTICAL GUIDE

provide a visual overview of complex data sets, making it easier for decision-makers to quickly grasp the insights and trends.

- **Customizable Data Views:** Allow users to customize the data views based on their specific needs and preferences. This can include filtering, sorting, or grouping data to allow users to focus on the most relevant information and gain insights quickly.
- **Real-time Data Updates:** Implement a system that allows data to be updated in real-time to provide up-to-date and accurate information. This can include automatic data refreshing, data streaming, or API integration to ensure that the displayed data is always current.
- **Data Driven Visualizations:** Use data-driven visualizations, such as charts, graphs, or heatmaps, that effectively convey complex information in a visually appealing and easy-to-understand manner. This can help users quickly grasp patterns, trends, and insights from the data.

Designing for large screens offers unique opportunities to create visually captivating and engaging experiences. By embracing the canvas, simplifying and focusing on key content, leveraging interactivity, considering the context of the environment, and testing and optimizing, you can create effective designs for large screens that leave a lasting impression on your audience.

Mastering Mobile Design

Mobile devices have become an integral part of our daily lives, and designing for mobile is thus a critical aspect of modern web design. With the proliferation of smartphones and tablets, users now expect seamless and engaging experiences on small screens. In this chapter, we will explore the principles and best practices of mobile design to create compelling and user-friendly mobile experiences.

Mobile design is the process of creating user interfaces and experiences that are optimized for small screens, touch interactions, and on-the-go usage. It involves designing for a smaller viewport, limited screen real estate, varying screen sizes, and different input methods.

Simplify and Prioritize Content: Mobile screens are small, and users have limited attention spans. It's crucial to simplify the content and prioritize the most important information to ensure a seamless and engaging experience. Avoid cluttering the screen with excessive text or visual elements, and focus on delivering the most relevant content to the user. Using concepts like progressive disclosure, where additional information is revealed as needed, can help keep the interface clean and uncluttered.

Responsive Design: Responsive design is a key approach to mobile design that ensures that websites and applications adapt to different screen sizes and orientations. It involves using flexible grids, fluid layouts, and media queries to adjust the layout and design elements based on the screen size, allowing for a consistent experience across various devices.

Clear and Intuitive Navigation: Navigation is a critical aspect of mobile design, and it needs to be clear, intuitive, and easy to use. Avoid complex menus or tiny buttons that are hard to tap, and consider using hamburger menus, tab bars, or other mobile-friendly navigation patterns. Also, provide feedback, such as highlighting the selected option, to give users visual cues about their current location within the app or website.

Optimize Touch Interactions: Mobile devices primarily rely on touch interactions, so it's crucial to optimize the design for touchscreens. Use larger buttons or interactive elements that are easy to tap with a finger, and provide enough spacing between elements to avoid accidental taps. Consider the ergonomics of the thumb, as most users hold their phones with one hand and use their thumb to interact with the screen.

Performance and Loading Speed: Mobile users are often on the go and may have limited internet connectivity, so it's essential to optimize the performance and loading speed of mobile designs. Optimize images, reduce HTTP requests, and minimize the use of animations or heavy scripts that could slow down the loading time. Also, consider using progressive loading techniques to provide a usable experience even when the network is slow.

How can UX Designers reduce HTTP Requests?

Optimize images: Compressing images and reducing their dimensions without sacrificing image quality can significantly reduce the file size and the number of HTTP requests required to load them.

Use icon fonts: Using icon fonts instead of images can help to reduce the number of HTTP requests required to load icons.

Consider SVG images: SVG images are vector-based, scalable, and can be created and manipulated using code. They can help to reduce HTTP requests by allowing designers to create graphics with fewer files.

Utilize reusable components: Designing with reusable components can reduce the number of HTTP requests by allowing developers to reuse elements throughout the design, rather than recreating them for each instance.

Consider Context and User Behavior: Mobile devices are used in various contexts, such as while commuting, standing in line, or on the couch. Consider the context and user behavior when designing for mobile, and provide solutions that fit seamlessly into their daily routine. For example, use location-based services, provide offline access, or leverage device capabilities, such as camera or accelerometer, to enhance the user experience.

Test and Iterate: Mobile design is an iterative process, and it's crucial to test the design on different devices, platforms, and network conditions to ensure a consistent and smooth experience. Use testing tools, conduct usability testing, and gather feedback from real users to identify any issues or areas for improvement, and iterate on the design accordingly.

Examples of Mobile Design Best Practices

- **Instagram:** Instagram's mobile app provides a clean and visually appealing interface that focuses on the core functionality of sharing and viewing photos. The navigation is simple, with a bottom tab bar for easy access to key features, and the touch interactions are optimized for swiping through images and scrolling through feeds. Instagram also uses progressive disclosure by hiding additional actions, such as liking or commenting on a post, behind icons that are revealed when the user interacts with a post.
- **Airbnb:** The Airbnb mobile app is designed with a strong focus on providing a seamless booking experience for travelers. The search and booking process is streamlined, with a simple and intuitive interface that

guides users through the steps. The app also uses location-based services to personalize search results and provide relevant recommendations. The use of large buttons and clear call-to-action (CTA) buttons makes it easy for users to book accommodations with minimal effort.

- **Google Maps:** Google Maps is a prime example of a mobile app that takes into consideration user behavior and context. It provides real-time location-based information, including directions, transit options, and local business information. The interface is designed with a clean and minimalistic approach, using progressive disclosure to reveal additional information as users interact with the map. The app also allows for offline access to maps, ensuring users can still access information even when they have limited connectivity.

Mobile design is a critical aspect of modern web design, and it's essential to create user-friendly and engaging experiences on small screens. By simplifying and prioritizing content, using responsive design, optimizing touch interactions, considering context and user behavior, and testing and iterating, designers can create compelling mobile experiences that meet the needs of today's mobile users. Applying principles such as progressive disclosure, clear navigation, and performance optimization can help create intuitive and seamless mobile designs that provide a positive user experience. With the ever-evolving landscape of mobile devices and user expectations, staying up-to-date with mobile design best practices is crucial for creating successful mobile experiences.

Designing for Wearables: Enhancing User Experience on Tiny Devices

Wearable devices, such as smartwatches, fitness trackers, and augmented reality (AR) glasses, have gained popularity in recent years due to their convenience, portability, and ability to provide real-time information. Designing for wearables presents unique challenges and opportunities, as the small screens and limited interactions require careful consideration of user experience (UX) principles. In this chapter, we will explore best practices for designing effective and engaging experiences for wearables, along with examples of successful wearable designs.

When designing for wearables, it's important to consider the context in which they are used. Wearable devices are typically worn on the body, and interactions are often quick and glanceable, with users relying on brief interactions to access information or perform actions. Therefore, the following best practices should be kept in mind:

- **Keep it simple:** Wearable devices have limited screen real estate, so it's crucial to simplify the interface and prioritize essential information.

Avoid cluttered screens or complex interactions that can overwhelm users.

- **Optimize for glanceability:** Users interact with wearables in brief, quick glances, so make sure that the information presented is easy to read and understand at a glance. Use clear and legible fonts, contrasting colors, and simple icons to convey information quickly.
- **Consider the physical form:** Wearable devices come in various forms, such as smartwatches, fitness bands, or AR glasses, and their physical attributes impact how users interact with them. For example, smart-watches are often worn on the wrist and require one-handed interactions, while AR glasses may have touch-sensitive frames or voice commands. Consider the form factor and physical interactions when designing for wearables.

Best Practices for Wearable Design

- **Focus on User Goals:** Design the wearable experience around the user's goals and needs. Understand the primary use case of the wearable device and prioritize features and content accordingly. Avoid unnecessary interactions or distractions that may hinder the user from achieving their goals.
- **Use Progressive Disclosure:** Due to the limited screen size of wearables, it's essential to use progressive disclosure, where information is revealed gradually as the user interacts with the device. This helps to reduce visual clutter and provide a more focused and seamless experience. For example, displaying only the most relevant information initially and allowing users to access additional details with further interactions.
- **Design for Quick Interactions:** Wearable devices are often used for quick interactions on the go, so make sure the interactions are easy, quick, and intuitive. Use large, touch-friendly buttons, simple gestures, or voice commands to facilitate interactions without requiring users to spend too much time or effort.
- **Leverage Sensors and Contextual Information:** Wearable devices often

have built-in sensors, such as heart rate monitors, accelerometers, or GPS, which can provide valuable contextual information. Use this information to personalize the user experience and provide relevant content or notifications based on the user's context or activity. For example, providing real-time fitness tracking data on a fitness band or displaying nearby points of interest on AR glasses.

- **Test and Iterate:** As with any UX design process, testing and iteration are crucial for designing successful wearable experiences. Conduct usability tests, gather feedback from users, and iterate on the design to improve usability and user satisfaction.

Examples of Successful Wearable Designs

- **Apple Watch:** Apple Watch is a popular smartwatch that exemplifies many of the best practices for wearable design. It uses a clean and simple interface with large, touch-friendly buttons and utilizes the digital crown for precise interactions. It also leverages sensors, such as heart rate monitors and GPS, to provide personalized health and fitness tracking features.
- **Fitbit:** Fitbit is a leading brand in the fitness tracker market, and their wearable devices are designed with a focus on simplicity and usability. The interface uses a minimalist design with clear fonts, simple icons, and large buttons for easy navigation. The devices also leverage sensors to track various health and fitness metrics, providing users with personalized feedback and insights.
- **Oculus Rift:** The Oculus Rift is a popular virtual reality headset that is designed to provide an immersive and interactive experience for users. Its design focuses on creating a realistic and immersive environment through the use of high-quality displays, precise head tracking, and intuitive hand controllers. The interface of the Oculus Rift is designed to be intuitive and easy to use, with menus and interactions that are optimized for virtual reality. Users can navigate through menus and options using hand gestures or controllers, making the experience feel

natural and intuitive.

The design of Oculus Rift also incorporates the concept of "presence," which refers to the feeling of being fully immersed in the virtual environment. The interface and interactions are designed to create a sense of presence, allowing users to interact with virtual objects and navigate through virtual environments as if they were physically there.

- **Snapchat Spectacles:** Snapchat Spectacles are a unique example of wearables designed specifically for capturing and sharing social media content. The sunglasses integrate a camera for recording short videos, which can be directly shared on Snapchat. The design of Spectacles focuses on simplicity and ease of use, with a single button for capturing videos and LED indicators to indicate recording status.
- **Garmin Venu:** Garmin Venu is a smartwatch designed for fitness enthusiasts, with a focus on health and fitness tracking features. The device has a vibrant AMOLED display that displays a wide range of fitness data, including heart rate, steps, sleep, and more. The interface uses large, easy-to-tap buttons and intuitive gestures for navigation, allowing users to access their fitness data quickly.

Responsive design and designing for different devices are crucial considerations in modern web design. By adopting responsive design techniques and incorporating device-specific UX principles, designers can ensure that their websites and applications are accessible, usable, and visually appealing across a wide range of devices, providing a seamless user experience regardless of the platform being used. Keeping up with the latest trends and best practices in responsive design and device-specific design will enable designers to create user-centric experiences that meet the needs of today's diverse and ever-evolving digital landscape.

* * *

Chapter 7: Technology Challenges

Welcome to the world of technology and user experience! As we explore the ever-evolving landscape of UX, it's important to acknowledge the impact of emerging technologies. From cutting-edge advancements in artificial intelligence and virtual reality to the latest gadgets and devices, technology is shaping how we interact with digital products and services in unprecedented ways.

But amidst the excitement of new possibilities, there lies a challenge that can't be ignored: legacy technology. Like that old dusty desktop computer in the corner of the office or the clunky software system that has been patched up more times than we can count, legacy technology is a reality that many UX professionals have to grapple with. And with it comes a unique set of UX challenges that can be frustrating, complex, and require creative problem-solving.

In UX design, **legacy technology** refers to outdated technology, software, hardware, or systems that can negatively impact the user experience. This technology can create obstacles for UX designers as they work to create modern and user-friendly interfaces. Legacy technology can limit the ability to incorporate new design trends or functionality that may enhance the user experience, and it can also create issues with compatibility and integration with newer technologies. UX designers must take into account any legacy technology that may be in use by their audience and design solutions that are compatible, accessible, and easy to use for all users, regardless of their technology background or experience. By doing so, UX designers can ensure a positive user experience and avoid potential barriers to adoption or engagement.

Design is a way of thinking, a way of solving problems.

Susan Weinschenk, behavioral scientist

In this chapter, we'll take a closer look at the tech challenges in UX, with a special focus on legacy technology. We'll explore how outdated systems and software, along with the remnants of a "band-aid" approach to adding new features without holistic redesign, can impact the user experience. We'll delve into the redundancies, repetitions, and inefficiencies that can arise from years of patchwork, and how UX professionals can navigate these challenges with ingenuity and resourcefulness. So, fasten your seatbelts, because we're about to dive into a world where floppy disks and dial-up internet still exist, and where UX designers are the unsung heroes untying the knots of outdated tech with clever solutions. Let's get started!

Tech-ing UX to the Next Level - An Exploration of Emerging Technologies in UX Design

As UX designers, we know that staying current with emerging technologies is key to creating innovative and engaging experiences. So let's dive into some of the most exciting tech trends that are shaking up the UX design world.

First up, **virtual and augmented reality (VR and AR)**. These technologies have been around for some time, but now they're more accessible and user-friendly than ever. With VR, users can be transported to a whole new world, while AR brings digital elements into the real world. Imagine testing out furniture in your own home with an AR app, or exploring a virtual museum exhibit. The possibilities for immersive experiences are endless.

Next, **artificial intelligence (AI)** is already being used in many areas of UX design, such as chatbots, voice assistants, and personalized recommendations. AI can also help predict user behavior, allowing designers to create even more personalized experiences. However, we must be careful not to rely too heavily on AI and neglect the importance of human-centered design.

Finally, the **Internet of Things (IoT)** is rapidly growing, with more and more devices becoming connected. This presents both challenges and opportunities for UX designers. The key is to create a seamless and intuitive experience that connects multiple devices and services in a meaningful way. Just think about the frustration of trying to set up a smart home system with incompatible devices - a seamless user experience is crucial.

But no matter how advanced our technology becomes, the fundamentals of good UX design remain the same. User-friendliness, accessibility, and intuitive design are still critical. And with the rapid pace of technological change, we must stay adaptable and flexible in our approach.

The future of UX design is exciting and full of potential. By embracing emerging technologies while remaining grounded in the principles of good UX design, we can create experiences that truly delight and engage users. So, let's tech UX to the next level!

Designing for Legacy Technology - Because Nothing Beats the Charm of Outdated Code

While it's exciting to talk about emerging technologies and cutting-edge design techniques, the reality is that many companies are still grappling with legacy systems and outdated technology.

Designing for legacy technology can be a daunting task. These outdated systems and applications can make any designer feel like they've been transported back to the dark ages of design. However, with careful planning and strategic updates, we can still create interfaces that are user-friendly and intuitive, even for those still stuck in the age of floppy disks and CRT monitors.

Compatibility is one of the biggest challenges of designing for legacy technology. These systems were designed to run on hardware and software configurations that are no longer available or supported. Updating them is like trying to fit a square peg into a round hole - it's not easy. But with the right approach, we can keep these systems functional for a few more years.

Another challenge is **user prioritization**. These old systems were often designed without a user-centric approach, resulting in interfaces that are clunky, confusing, and just plain frustrating. But with a little bit of creativity and a lot of empathy, we can create interfaces that are as intuitive and streamlined as possible, despite the limitations of the system.

And finally, there's the issue of maintenance and support. Legacy systems often require specialized knowledge and expertise to maintain, which can be a challenge for companies trying to move away from these systems. But with a little bit of foresight and planning, we can design interfaces that are easy to maintain and support, even for those with limited experience with legacy technology.

The Frustrating Joy of Improving Legacy Products

Legacy technology is not the only challenge that UX designers face; legacy user experience (UX) can be just as daunting. When dealing with legacy UX, designers are often confronted with products that were built over time, with new features added in a bandaid-like manner that can make them clunky and non-user-friendly.

Adding new features to a product in a haphazard way can lead to a plethora of design issues, resulting in a system that is difficult to use and can cause frustration for users. These issues can stem from the dozens of bandaids that have been applied over time to patch up the product's holes.

> Legacy technology is not an excuse for poor user experience. It's an opportunity for UX designers to challenge the status quo and find innovative ways to improve the user experience.
>
> Unknown

One of the biggest challenges for UX designers dealing with legacy UX is convincing leadership to overhaul a large, currently used product. Redesigning the product in its entirety can be disruptive and requires significant resources. Additionally, there may be resistance from customers who have grown accustomed to the product's current state and may not be keen on learning a new system. However, despite these challenges, customers are still asking for more modern features and are complaining about clunky design. To meet these demands, UX designers need to be strategic in their approach.

Let's face it, dealing with legacy UX can feel like trying to untangle a giant ball of yarn that your cat has been playing with for days. It's messy, frustrating, and can leave you wanting to scream into a pillow. But fear not, my fellow UX designers, there are a few tips and tricks we can use to tackle this problem. Here are some actionable steps you can take:

- **Focus on the low-hanging fruit:** Start by addressing the small changes that can make a big difference. Can you improve the font size? Add more white space? Simplify the navigation? These changes can make a noticeable impact on the user experience without requiring a complete overhaul.
- **Identify the critical pain points:** Work with your team to identify the biggest pain points for users. These are the areas where you can make the most significant impact. Start by fixing these issues and gradually work towards updating the rest of the system.
- **Utilize design patterns:** Don't reinvent the wheel! Utilize existing design patterns that are familiar to users. This will help them feel more comfortable with the changes you're making, even if they're small.
- **Collaborate with the development team:** The developers know the system inside and out. Work with them to understand the limitations of the technology and find ways to make the necessary improvements without breaking the system.

Resistance to Change in UX - "Why Won't They Let Us Make Things Better?"

As a UX professional, you may find yourself in a situation where you face resistance to change from different stakeholders, including the big bosses, developers, and even users. The stakeholders may refuse to change the old interface out of fear of losing their "legacy job security."

Resistance to change can be a real pain in the behind for UX designers. It can prevent the adoption of innovative design solutions that can improve the user experience, leaving everyone frustrated with the status quo. But why won't they let us make things better?

Well, there are several reasons why people resist change in UX design. Some people may have a vested interest in the existing design, like developers who don't want to learn a new language or executives who don't want to spend more money. Others may not understand the need for change or fear that change will disrupt their workflows or make their jobs more difficult. It's like trying to convince a toddler to eat their vegetables instead of candy.

So, how can you overcome resistance to change in UX design? First, it's essential to **communicate the benefits** of the proposed changes in a way that stakeholders can understand. Use pictures, analogies, and memes if you have to. Involve stakeholders in the design process, providing them with a sense of ownership and engagement in the project. This way, they'll be more likely to understand the need for change and support the new design.

Another way to overcome resistance to change is to **provide training and support** to stakeholders. Developers may need training on new design tools, while users may need guidance on how to use the new interface effectively. It's like teaching your grandma how to use Facebook, but without the frustration. By providing adequate training and support, you can help stakeholders feel more confident and comfortable with the changes, reducing their resistance.

It's also essential to **address the emotional side of resistance to change**. People may feel threatened or anxious about the proposed changes, and it's essential to acknowledge and address these concerns. Listening to their feedback and providing a space for discussion can help to build trust and understanding. It's like a therapy session, but for UX designers and stakeholders.

Finally, it's important to recognize that **resistance to change is a natural part of the design process**. Not every design solution will be immediately accepted, and it's important to remain flexible and open to feedback. By engaging with stakeholders, providing training and support, and addressing their emotional concerns, you can help to overcome resistance to change and create innovative, user-centered designs that will make everyone happy.

Additional Challenges of Dealing with Legacy UX

In addition to the challenges of outdated technology and resistance to change, there are several other aspects of dealing with legacy UX that can make the design process more difficult.

One common challenge is a **lack of documentation**. When dealing with a legacy product, it's not uncommon to find that there is little or no documentation of the original design or development process. This can make it difficult for UX designers to understand the reasoning behind certain design decisions, or to identify the root causes of design issues.

Another challenge is the **need to maintain backward compatibility**. When updating a legacy product, it's important to ensure that the new design is compatible with existing workflows, data formats, and other aspects of the system. This can be particularly challenging when dealing with legacy systems that may have been designed decades ago.

In some cases, the legacy UX may have been **designed with outdated or**

incorrect assumptions about user behavior or preferences. For example, a legacy system may have been designed for a specific user demographic or with assumptions about the available technology that are no longer accurate. In these cases, UX designers must work to identify and correct these assumptions to ensure that the new design is user-centered and effective.

Finally, it's worth noting that **dealing with legacy UX can be emotionally challenging** for UX designers. It can be frustrating to work with a system that is outdated or difficult to use, particularly when the designer is aware of the potential improvements that could be made. In some cases, designers may even feel a sense of nostalgia or attachment to the legacy system, further complicating the design process.

To address these additional challenges of dealing with legacy UX, designers must remain flexible, creative, and persistent. They should be prepared to work with limited documentation, and to communicate clearly with stakeholders about the need for changes. Additionally, they must remain aware of the need for backward compatibility and the potential for outdated assumptions in the legacy products. By remaining focused on the needs of the user and maintaining a user-centered design approach, UX designers can successfully overcome these challenges and create effective, modern user experiences.

* * *

Chapter 8: UX vs. Silos - Breaking Down Barriers

Organizational silos occur when different departments or teams within a company operate independently and don't share information or resources. A grain silo on a farm can be used as an analogy to explain organizational silos. Just as a grain silo is used to store specific types of grains and keep them separate from each other, departments in a company may operate in silos, focusing on their own objectives and keeping information to themselves.

For example, the marketing team may focus solely on advertising and promotions, while the engineering team may be focused on product development. They may have different goals and metrics for success, which can create communication gaps and inefficiencies. This can lead to missed opportunities and slower progress towards company-wide goals.

Breaking down organizational silos can be compared to breaking down the walls of a grain silo. Just as farmers may need to remove the walls of a grain silo to mix different types of grains, a company may need to create cross-functional teams to ensure that different departments are working together towards common goals. This can promote collaboration, knowledge-sharing, and a better understanding of the overall company strategy.

Ultimately, breaking down silos requires a shift in mindset and a willingness to collaborate across teams. Just like the farmer who mixes different types of grains to create a better crop yield, a company that breaks down organizational silos can create a stronger, more efficient organization that can achieve its goals more effectively.

Breaking down Silos with Potluck Design

In many organizations, silos can be a major obstacle to effective UX design. But fear not, because there's a delicious solution to this problem: potluck design.

Just like a potluck dinner, where everyone brings their own dish to share and creates a delicious meal together, potluck design involves creating cross-functional teams that include representatives from each department. This ensures that everyone has a seat at the table and can contribute to the design process. But how do you make sure everyone brings something tasty to the potluck? Here are some tips:

- **Encourage collaboration:** Set up a collaborative environment that encourages everyone to work together and share their ideas. Make sure that everyone feels valued and heard, and that no one dominates the conversation.
- **Be open-minded:** Don't be afraid to try new things and experiment with different ideas. Be open-minded and willing to take risks, and encourage others to do the same.
- **Provide structure:** Establish clear goals and objectives for the project, and provide structure and guidelines to help keep everyone on track. This will help to ensure that the potluck design process is focused and productive.
- **Celebrate success:** Finally, make sure to celebrate the success of the potluck design process. Take time to acknowledge everyone's contributions, and celebrate the final product together as a team.

Playing on the Same Team: Creating a Shared Vision for UX

In UX, a shared vision is crucial for success. When different teams or departments have conflicting priorities, it can lead to a lack of coherence and result in a suboptimal user experience. To ensure a shared vision in UX, it's essential to involve all stakeholders in the process. This means inviting representatives from each department to share their perspectives and ideas to create a consensus where everyone feels valued and heard.

Next, a set of specific and measurable goals should be established that align with overall business objectives. Regular communication is key to ensure all stakeholders are updated on progress and can offer feedback and input.

Creating a set of UX guidelines or standards can also promote a shared vision. Having a playbook of sorts can ensure all teams are working towards the same principles and design standards. Celebrating wins and successes along the way and recognizing individuals or teams that contributed to the shared goals can also help create a sense of unity.

Ultimately, creating a shared vision in UX is about working as a team towards a common goal.

Breaking Down Organizational Silos with a Unified Design System

In a world of organizational silos, a unified design system can be the ultimate weapon for UX professionals. It's like a superhero team where everyone has their unique powers, but they work together to save the day. By creating a shared library of design patterns, components, and guidelines, everyone in the organization can work towards the same design goals. This not only creates consistency in products but also speeds up development time, saving valuable resources.

Tips for building a Design System:

· **Start with a strong foundation:** A design system should have a solid foundation of typography, colors, and layout principles. These foundational elements should be consistent and cohesive across all products and platforms.

137

- **Use design tokens:** Use design tokens to define the colors, typography, spacing, and other design elements that will be used throughout your product. This will ensure consistency and make it easier to make global changes to your design system.
- **Prioritize accessibility:** Make sure your design system is accessible by following best practices for color contrast, text size, and other accessibility guidelines. This will ensure that your product can be used by all users, regardless of their abilities.
- **Test responsiveness:** Ensure that your design system is responsive by testing it on different screen sizes and devices. This will ensure that your product looks good and functions properly on all devices.
- **Get feedback and update regularly:** Collect feedback from users and update your design system regularly to address any issues and improve the overall user experience.
- **Use the design system across different projects:** Use your design system across different types of projects early on to ensure its applicability and make any necessary adjustments. This will help ensure consistency across all of your products and make it easier to create new designs in the future.

One of the biggest benefits of a unified design system is the elimination of redundancies. By having a centralized design system, features like the login process can be done once and shared across multiple products. This creates a better UX across the products and can save users time and frustration. Additionally, a unified design system can help break down organizational silos by providing a common language for design. No more debates over which shade of blue to use or which font to choose. The design system provides a clear framework for making these decisions, reducing the risk of conflicting priorities.

By implementing a unified design system, UX professionals can optimize product performance and create a compelling case for senior leadership. It's like hitting a home run in the championship game. When everyone works together towards a common goal, the results can be truly amazing.

* * *

Chapter 9: Navigating the Sea of Stakeholders

When it comes to UX design, schools often teach that the primary focus should be on the user. But in reality, there are a whole bunch of other stakeholders that can make a UX designer's life a living nightmare. Let's take a look at some of the most common ones.

First up, we have the **client**. This is the person or organization that is paying for the product or service you're designing. They might have a vision for what they want the product to be, but they probably have no idea what actually makes for a good user experience. And they might change their mind about what they want at any moment, forcing you to start from scratch.

Next, we have the **executives**. These are the people who are ultimately responsible for the success or failure of the product. They may not have any expertise in UX design, but they're the ones making the final decisions about what gets shipped. And if something goes wrong, they'll be the first to point the finger.

Then there are the **marketers**. They're the ones who have to sell the product to the masses, so they'll want flashy features and a catchy slogan. They might not care so much about usability or accessibility, as long as they can make it look good in a TV commercial.

And let's not forget about the **engineers**. They're the ones who have to build the thing, and they'll have plenty of opinions about what's feasible and what's not. They may not comprehend why a particular design choice is crucial for the user, but they will definitely inform you if it's difficult to code.

There are also the **legal and compliance folks**. They're the ones who make sure the product doesn't violate any laws or regulations. They might not care about the user experience at all, as long as the product doesn't get the company sued.

Last but not least, there are the **users** themselves. They're the reason we're all here, right? Well, they're also the ones who can make or break the product with their feedback. They might not know what they want until they see it, and they might not be able to articulate their frustrations with the product in a way that's helpful to you.

When it comes to UX design, you're not just designing for the user. You're also designing for a whole bunch of other stakeholders who might not have the user's best interests at heart. It can be a tricky balancing act, but if you can navigate the sea of stakeholders with finesse, you just might end up with a product that everyone is happy with (or at least, not too unhappy).

Navigating the Turbulent Waters of Client Management

Dealing with clients is a bit like navigating a ship through a stormy sea - you never know what's going to hit you next. One moment, they're thrilled with your design, and the next, they're demanding a complete overhaul because their niece's dog doesn't like the color scheme.

To make matters worse, clients often have no idea what they want. They might have a vague concept in mind, like "something that pops," or "something more modern," but they can't articulate how that should be achieved. And don't even get me started on the clients who want to copy their competitor's design, but with a different logo. As a UX designer, it's your job to educate your client on what makes for a good user experience. But when your client thinks that "user experience" means giving their users as many options as possible, or bombarding them with ads, it can be an uphill battle.

So, how can you manage your clients effectively? Firstly, you need to be able to **communicate your design decisions** clearly and persuasively. Use data and research to back up your choices, and be prepared to explain the reasoning behind your design. But don't expect this to be a one-and-done deal - you might need to reiterate your rationale several times before it sinks in.

Secondly, you need to be **prepared to handle the inevitable changes in scope** and direction. Remember, your client is the one paying the bills, so their whims and fancies take precedence. But that doesn't mean you have to be a doormat - set clear boundaries and expectations from the outset, and be prepared to negotiate when changes inevitably arise.

Lastly, don't forget to take care of yourself. **Dealing with difficult clients can be emotionally draining**, so make sure to schedule breaks and prioritize self-care. And remember, there's always a light at the end of the tunnel -

eventually, the project will be over, and you can look back on it as a learning experience (or a cautionary tale).

The Art of Winning Over Executives: A Guide for UX Designers

When it comes to stakeholders, executives hold a special place in the hearts of UX designers. These are the individuals who call the shots, make the final decisions, and ultimately determine the success or failure of a project. While they may not have any expertise in UX design, they are the ones with the power and influence to shape the product. As a result, dealing with executives can be a delicate dance of catering to their needs while also advocating for the user experience.

As a UX designer, you might think your job is to create a product that works well and is enjoyable to use. But let's be real, your job is to make the executives happy. They're the ones signing the checks, after all. But how do you deal with these all-powerful stakeholders? Here are a few tips:

- **Speak their language:** Executives love buzzwords and acronyms. Throw in a few "ROI"s and "KPI"s, and they'll be eating out of your hand.

- **Make it look pretty:** If your design looks good, the executives will assume it works well. And if it doesn't, well, at least it looks good.
- **Keep it simple:** Executives don't have time for complexity. They want to know what the product does and how it's going to make them money. If you can explain that in a few bullet points, you're golden.
- **Be confident:** Executives respect confidence, even if it's misplaced. If you can talk a good game and look like you know what you're doing, they'll trust you.

Of course, these tips are a bit tongue-in-cheek. But the truth is, dealing with executives can be a challenge. They may not understand the intricacies of UX design, but they do understand the bottom line. So, if you can show them how your work is going to make them money, they'll be happy. And if you can make it look good at the same time, all the better.

> **ROI** stands for "**return on investment**." It's a way of measuring how much money you make back after you spend money on something. So, if you invest $100 in something and it makes you $150, then your ROI is 50%. It helps you understand whether something is a good investment or not.

Marketers: Making UX Design a Selling Point

Ah, the marketers. The masters of spin, the lords of hype. They can sell anything to anyone, as long as they have a good story to tell. And when it comes to UX design, they're always looking for ways to make it a selling point.

As a UX designer, you might think your job is to create a product that works well and is enjoyable to use. But in the eyes of the marketers, your job is to create a product that can be sold. And that means focusing on the features and benefits that will appeal to the masses. But how do you deal with these savvy salespeople? Here are a few tips:

- **Focus on the sizzle, not the steak:** Marketers love flashy features and bells and whistles. If you can make your design look cool and cutting-edge, they'll be all over it.
- **Make it sound exciting:** Marketers want to create buzz and excitement around the product. Use words like "revolutionary," "game-changing," and "innovative" to get them excited.
- **Highlight the benefits:** Marketers are all about the benefits of a product, not the features. Make sure you can explain how your design will improve people's lives or make them more productive.
- **Be ready to compromise:** Marketers are always looking for ways to differentiate the product from the competition. Be prepared to make changes or add features that may not align with your UX design principles.
- **Embrace the jargon:** Marketers love buzzwords and industry jargon. If

you can talk the talk, they'll be more likely to respect your expertise.

While these tips may come across as humorous, the reality is that working with marketers can sometimes be difficult. Their focus is often on telling a compelling story to promote a product or service, rather than the finer details of UX design. By working with them to create a narrative that showcases the value of your design, you can help them better understand the importance of your work. This collaboration might even result in your design becoming a viral hit.

When Engineers Meet UX Designers: A Clash of the Titans

As a UX designer, you might think your job is to create a product that's easy to use and meets the needs of the user. But what do those pesky engineers think? They're the ones who have to make your designs a reality, and they're not always happy about it.

To engineers, usability is just one factor to consider. They have to think about things like scalability, maintainability, and performance. And they'll be the first to point out if your design is going to cause problems down the line. So, how do you deal with these tech-minded stakeholders? Here are a few tips:

- **Speak their language:** Engineers love technical jargon and acronyms. Throw in a few "APIs" and "MVCs," and they'll be impressed with your knowledge.
- **Be realistic:** Engineers deal with practical problems all the time, so they're not going to be impressed with pie-in-the-sky designs that are impossible to implement.
- **Be open to feedback:** Engineers have a lot of expertise, so don't be afraid to listen to their opinions. They might have insights that you haven't considered.
- **Be patient:** Engineers can be notoriously difficult to work with, so don't take their criticisms personally. Remember that you're both on the same team, and try to find a way to work together.

Of course, these tips are easier said than done. Engineers and UX designers have very different mindsets, and it can be a challenge to find common ground. But if you can bridge the gap between design and implementation, you'll have a much better chance of creating a product that's both usable and technically sound.

APIs (Application Programming Interfaces): APIs are like sets of instructions that allow different software applications to communicate and interact with each other. They define a way for one program to request data or perform actions from another program, making it easier for different apps or systems to work together and share information.

MVCs (Model-View-Controller): MVC is a design pattern used in software development to organize and structure code in a way that separates different parts of an application. The "Model" represents the data and logic of the application, the "View" displays the information to the user, and the "Controller" handles user input and manages the interaction between the Model and the View. It's like a way of dividing the work in a software application so that it's easier to understand and maintain. Think of it as a team of superheroes where each member has a specific role to play to save the day!

The Law and the User: Balancing Legal Compliance and UX Design

UX designers have a clear goal in mind: to create a product that meets user needs and delights them in the process. But there's another stakeholder in the mix: legal and compliance teams. While they may not have the same user-centric focus, they play a crucial role in ensuring that the product doesn't land the company in legal hot water.

For UX designers, this can be a delicate balancing act. On one hand, they want to create an experience that users will love. On the other hand, they need to make sure that experience is legally compliant. This can mean jumping through hoops to accommodate laws and regulations that might seem counterintuitive or downright frustrating. For example, a design choice that seems like a no-brainer from a UX perspective might run afoul of accessibility laws. Or, a feature that users love might have to be redesigned due to privacy concerns. Navigating these challenges can require a lot of back-and-forth with legal and compliance teams and can sometimes lead to compromises that feel less than ideal. But in the end, the product needs to meet both user needs and legal requirements.

So, what's a UX designer to do? One approach is to **proactively involve legal and compliance teams in the design process**. This can help ensure that potential legal issues are caught early on, before they become major roadblocks. It can also help build trust and understanding between teams, making it easier to collaborate in the long run.

Another approach is to **stay up-to-date on relevant laws and regulations**, and to incorporate them into design decisions from the outset. This can help minimize surprises down the line, and can also signal to legal and compliance teams that UX designers are taking their concerns seriously.

Ultimately, creating a great user experience while staying legally compliant is no small feat. It requires a willingness to collaborate, a deep understanding of both user needs and legal requirements, and a healthy dose of creativity. But with the right mindset and approach, it's possible to meet both goals and create a product that everyone can be proud of.

The Unpredictable Users: When Feedback Becomes a Nightmare

Users, the people we design for and the ones who hold the key to the success or failure of our product. It's our job to please them, but it's easier said than done. Users can be fickle, unpredictable creatures who don't always know what they want until they see it.

As UX designers, we want to create a product that's intuitive, enjoyable, and solves a real problem for our users. But sometimes, users can make our job a real nightmare. They might provide feedback that's contradictory or doesn't make sense. Or worse, they might not provide any feedback at all, leaving us in the dark about what's working and what's not.

And let's not forget about user testing. It's a crucial part of the design process, but it can also be a real challenge. Users might not know how to articulate their frustrations with the product, or they might not want to hurt our feelings by giving negative feedback. And even if we get good feedback, implementing it can be a whole other challenge. We might not have the time or resources to make all the changes users want, or we might have to compromise on some things in order to meet other stakeholders' needs. So how do we deal with these unpredictable users? Here are a few tips:

- **Encourage honest feedback:** Let users know that you want to hear their thoughts, even if they're negative. Create a safe space for feedback where users feel comfortable sharing their thoughts.
- **Use different methods of user testing:** Don't rely solely on surveys or interviews. Try different methods like user observation or A/B testing to get a better understanding of how users are interacting with your product.
- **Don't take feedback personally:** Remember that feedback is not a personal attack. Users are not criticizing you; they're criticizing the product. Take feedback as an opportunity to improve, not as a personal insult.
- **Prioritize feedback:** Not all feedback is created equal. Prioritize the feedback that's going to have the biggest impact on the user experience or on meeting stakeholders' needs.

In the end, dealing with users can be a real challenge, but it's also what makes our job as UX designers so rewarding. If we can create a product that truly meets our user's needs and delights them in the process, it's all worth it.

User observation is when UX designers watch how people use a product or service to learn what works well and what doesn't. This helps designers make improvements that make the product easier and more enjoyable to use.

A/B testing is a way to test two versions of something, like a website or an app, to see which one works better. It's like when you try two different ice cream flavors to decide which one you like more. With A/B testing, you can try different designs, colors, or wording to see which one people like more. This helps make sure that the final product is the best it can be for the people who will use it.

REAL UX: PRACTICAL GUIDE

* * *

Chapter 10: Embracing Quality in UX Design

I n the world of UX design, quality is king. It is the cornerstone of every successful product, the measure by which all others are judged. But what is quality in UX design, and how can it be achieved?

At its core, quality in UX design refers to the degree to which a product meets the needs and expectations of its users. A high-quality product is one that is intuitive, user-friendly, and efficient, with a design that is aesthetically pleasing and visually appealing. Achieving quality in UX design requires a combination of skill, experience, and attention to detail, as well as a deep understanding of the needs and expectations of the product's target audience.

One of the key concepts in achieving quality in UX design is the idea of "quality through quantity." This concept is based on the idea that the more iterations of a design a UX designer creates, the more opportunities they have to identify and address flaws in the design. By creating many mockups and prototypes, designers can experiment with different solutions, evaluate the results, and refine their design until it meets the desired level of quality.

Let's explore some tips for achieving quality in UX design and how to incorporate the concept of quality through quantity into your design process.

The Story of Quality and Quantity

In the book "Art & Fear" by David Bayles and Ted Orland, there is a story about a ceramics teacher who divided his class into two groups: one graded on the quantity of work they produced, and the other on the quality of their work. The quantity group was tasked with producing as much work as possible, while the quality group was tasked with producing only one perfect piece.

On the final day of class, the ceramics teacher weighed the work of the quantity group and assigned grades based on the weight of their creations. The quality group only had to produce one perfect piece to receive an "A."

Interestingly, when the grades were tallied, the works of the highest quality were all produced by the quantity group. **While the quality group was busy theorizing and striving for perfection, the quantity group was busily churning out work, making mistakes and learning from them, resulting in a higher level of quality in their work.**

This story is a great example of the **quality through quantity** concept. It highlights the importance of producing a large quantity of work in order to learn from mistakes, iterate on designs, and ultimately achieve a higher level of quality. In UX design, this means creating many mockups and prototypes to test different solutions and evaluate which ones work best for the users.

But quantity alone is not enough to achieve quality. It's important to approach each mockup with a critical eye and strive to improve upon each iteration. In the next section, we will explore some tips and techniques for achieving quality in UX design.

Achieving Quality in UX Design

Quality is a critical aspect of UX design. A high-quality user experience is what separates successful products from those that fail. However, achieving quality is not an easy feat. It requires a combination of skills, processes, and techniques to create a design that meets the needs of the users and achieves the business goals.

The concept of "quality through quantity," as illustrated in the story from Art & Fear, can be an effective technique to achieve quality. However, this approach only works if designers learn from their mistakes. Simply producing a large quantity of low-quality designs won't be helpful. By creating a significant volume of work, designers can refine and iterate their designs, recognize their shortcomings, and improve the overall quality of their output. This technique provides an opportunity for designers to experiment with various concepts and methods, test them with users, and pinpoint the most effective solution.

> "Good design is like a refrigerator—when it works, no one notices, but when it doesn't, it sure stinks."
>
> Irene Au, Silicon Valley designer and design leader

Another way to achieve quality is through **collaboration**. By working with a team of designers, developers, and stakeholders, designers can gain different perspectives and insights that can help improve the design. Collaboration also helps ensure that everyone is working towards the same goal and that the design is meeting the needs of both the users and the business.

Usability testing is another essential technique for achieving quality. By testing the design with real users, designers can identify usability issues and areas for improvement. This feedback can then be used to iterate and refine the design, resulting in a higher quality product.

Finally, **attention to detail** is crucial for achieving quality in UX design. The design should be consistent, easy to use, and visually appealing. Small details like typography, spacing, and color can make a big difference in the user experience. Therefore, it's essential to pay attention to every aspect of the design and ensure that it meets the highest standards of quality.

* * *

Chapter 11: UX Across Different Company Sizes

C rafting seamless user experiences in different companies of varying sizes presents unique challenges for UX designers. Each organization, whether it be a small startup or a large enterprise, has its own set of hurdles that require creative solutions.

Let's take a closer look at some of the UX challenges and strategies for success based on the size of the company:

Startups: The Daredevil Dilemma

In startups, the pace is fast, and resources are often limited. UX designers may face challenges such as limited budgets, tight deadlines, and competing priorities. However, this can also be an opportunity for creativity and innovation. Strategies may include prioritizing the most critical user flows, leveraging rapid prototyping and user feedback, and advocating for the value of UX to stakeholders.

Small and Medium-sized Enterprises (SMEs): The Balancing Act

In SMEs, UX designers may face the challenge of striking a balance between user-centric design and business goals. Budget constraints and decision-making processes can impact UX efforts. Strategies may include building a business case for UX, collaborating with cross-functional teams, and leveraging existing design systems or frameworks to streamline the process.

Large Enterprises: The Juggling Act

In large enterprises, UX designers may encounter challenges such as organizational complexity, siloed teams, and legacy systems. Navigating corporate politics and aligning diverse stakeholders can be a juggling act. Strategies may include building relationships with key decision-makers, advocating for UX best practices, and leveraging user data and analytics to make data-driven design decisions.

Global Companies: The Localization Maze

In global companies, UX designers may face the challenge of designing for diverse cultures, languages, and markets. Adapting the user experience to local preferences, customs, and accessibility standards can be complex. Strategies may include conducting thorough user research in local markets, partnering with local teams, and leveraging localization tools and best practices.

Consulting or Agency: The Chameleon Approach

In consulting or agency settings, UX designers may need to adapt to different clients, industries, and project requirements. Each project may have its own unique challenges and constraints. Strategies may include being adaptable and flexible, understanding the client's business goals and user needs, and collaborating closely with clients to deliver tailored solutions.

Regardless of the company size, UX designers need to be agile, adaptable, and strategic in their approach. It's about finding the right balance between user-centric design, business goals, and organizational dynamics. So, let's gear up and get ready to scale the UX mountain, navigating the challenges of designing delightful user experiences in companies of different sizes! After all, every design journey requires skilled navigation to overcome the unique terrain of UX design in diverse organizational settings. Let's embark on this adventure with confidence and creativity, ready to conquer any obstacles that come our way! Let's get started!

UX and the Startup Rollercoaster: Buckle Up for a Wild Ride

Ah, the world of startups. Are you considering working for a startup? Well, let me tell you about the ups and downs, twists and turns, and all the quirks that come with working in a small, scrappy company.

Advantages

- Startups offer the opportunity to wear multiple hats and gain experience in a variety of roles, such as UX designer, project manager, and product owner, which can lead to accelerated professional growth and development.
- Working in a small team can foster a sense of community and camaraderie, where everyone is working towards a common goal and can have a significant impact on the organization's success.
- Startups often have a flat organizational structure, which can provide more direct access to decision-makers, executives, and founders, allowing for faster decision-making and the ability to influence the direction of the company.

- With a leaner budget, startups may be more willing to take risks and try new things, providing UX designers with the opportunity to experiment and innovate in their designs.

Disadvantages

- Uncertainty is a significant downside to working for a startup. The startup world is inherently risky, with no guarantee of success, stability, or longevity. This instability can create anxiety and stress for employees.
- With limited resources, startups may not have access to the latest design tools, software, or technologies, which can create challenges for UX designers trying to create optimal user experiences.
- The pressure to perform can be high, with the need to deliver results quickly and efficiently to keep the company afloat. This can lead to long hours and a lack of work-life balance.
- Due to the fast-paced nature of startups, the design process can be chaotic, with constantly changing priorities and goals, which can make it challenging to establish a consistent design language and maintain coherence across different products and services.

On the bright side, working for a startup can be a playground for your creativity. You'll have the opportunity to work with brilliant minds who also happen to be total weirdos. I'm talking about the guy who wears a cowboy hat to work every day or the girl who eats nothing but kale and avocado toast. And don't be surprised if the office looks like a cross between a kindergarten classroom and a tech lab. Bean bag chairs, ping pong tables, and post-it notes galore.

Tips for Tackling UX Challenges in a Startup

- **Prioritize:** In a small company environment, resources can be limited, so it's essential to prioritize UX efforts. Focus on the most critical user flows and features first, and work with stakeholders to determine the areas that will have the most significant impact on the user experience.
- **Leverage Rapid Prototyping and User Feedback:** Rapid prototyping and user feedback can be particularly valuable in a startup environment. Use prototypes to test and validate UX designs quickly, and use feedback to iterate and refine your design.
- **Advocate for UX:** As a UX designer in a small company, you'll need to advocate for the value of UX to stakeholders who may not understand its importance. Communicate the impact of UX on user engagement and the company's success, and use data to back up your claims.
- **Be Agile:** In a startup environment, the development process is often agile, which means you'll need to be flexible and adaptable. Stay open to feedback and willing to pivot when necessary, and be prepared to wear multiple hats and take on new challenges as they arise.

Working for a startup can be a wild ride, but if you're up for the challenge, it can be worth it. You'll never be bored, that's for sure. And when it comes to UX challenges, don't be afraid to take risks and try new things. Who knows, you might come up with the next big thing. Just keep some Advil nearby for those inevitable headaches.

So if you're a UX designer looking for a little adventure, the startup world might just be the place for you. Just remember to buckle up, hold on tight, and enjoy the ride. Who knows where it might take you!

SMEs: UX Design on a Tightrope

UX designers in **small and medium-sized enterprises (SMEs)** are like acrobats on a tightrope. They need to balance business goals with user-centric design without falling off. It's not an easy feat, but it's worth it for those who are up for the challenge.

Advantages

- Working in an SME allows UX designers to have a greater impact on the organization's success, as they have the opportunity to work in cross-functional teams and influence decision-making. This can lead to a sense of purpose and ownership over their work.
- With flatter hierarchies, UX designers in SMEs can take on more responsibility and have more control over their work, which can lead to accelerated professional growth and development.
- The flexibility that SMEs can offer, such as remote work or flexible hours, can be a major perk for UX designers who value work-life balance.
- SMEs may have a smaller user base, but this can be an advantage as UX designers can build closer relationships with users and gain a deep understanding of their needs and behaviors. This can lead to more

personalized and effective designs.

Disadvantages

- Limited resources for UX research, prototyping, or testing can be a major challenge in SMEs. UX designers may need to be more resourceful and creative in finding ways to conduct research and validate their designs.
- Unclear decision-making processes can be a significant disadvantage in SMEs, as it can be challenging to get buy-in for UX initiatives or to get feedback on design decisions. This can require UX designers to be more proactive in communicating their ideas and building consensus.
- The smaller team size in SMEs can foster a sense of community and camaraderie, but it can also lead to overwork and burnout, as there may be fewer resources to share the workload.
- The fast-paced nature of SMEs can create chaos in the design process, with constantly changing priorities and goals, which can make it challenging to establish a consistent design language and maintain coherence across different products and services.

Tips for UX designers

- **Build a business case:** To get buy-in for UX initiatives, UX designers need to build a business case that shows how UX can benefit the company's overall goals and objectives.
- **Collaborate with cross-functional teams:** Work closely with other teams, such as marketing, development, or product management, to ensure that UX aligns with their goals and objectives.
- **Leverage existing design systems or frameworks:** SMEs may not have the budget or resources to build a design system from scratch. Therefore, leveraging existing frameworks or design systems can help streamline the UX process and ensure consistency across the product or service.

By striking a balance between user-centric design and business goals, UX designers in SMEs can create products and services that not only meet user needs but also align with the company's objectives.

Large Enterprises: A UX Designer's Epic Odyssey

In large enterprises, UX designers embark on an epic journey to create user-centered designs while navigating through organizational hierarchies, competing priorities, and the occasional monster lurking in legacy systems. It's a challenging journey, but with the right strategies and tools, UX designers can make a significant impact and help users reach their destination.

Advantages

- With access to a vast pool of resources, such as budgets, teams, and technology, UX designers can create designs that cater to the needs of a broad audience and have a significant impact on the organization's success.

- Exposure to diverse stakeholders, including executives, product managers, and subject matter experts, can provide UX designers with valuable insights and help them create designs that align with the organization's goals.
- Opportunities to work on high-impact projects that can reach a vast audience can help UX designers showcase their skills and advance their careers.

Disadvantages

- Organizational complexity can make it difficult to implement user-centric design practices, streamline workflows, and get buy-in for UX initiatives.
- Siloed teams and legacy systems can slow down the design process and create roadblocks that UX designers need to overcome.
- The large scale of the organization can make it challenging to maintain consistency in design and user experience across different products and services, which can lead to confusion and frustration for users.

Tips for Designers

- **Build relationships with key decision-makers:** In large enterprises, it is crucial to establish strong relationships with executives and other key decision-makers to advocate for UX best practices and ensure that user needs are taken into account in decision-making processes.
- **Advocate for UX best practices:** It can be challenging to get stakeholders to prioritize UX in large enterprises. UX designers must be proactive in educating stakeholders about the value of UX and advocating for user-centric design practices.
- **Leverage user data and analytics:** In large enterprises, there is often an abundance of user data and analytics available. UX designers can use this data to make data-driven design decisions and demonstrate the impact of UX on business goals.

- **Collaborate with cross-functional teams:** UX designers should collaborate with cross-functional teams, such as developers, product managers, and subject matter experts, to ensure that design decisions are aligned with business goals and user needs.
- **Streamline workflows:** Large enterprises can be bogged down by bureaucracy and slow decision-making processes. UX designers can streamline workflows by leveraging existing design systems or frameworks to ensure consistency and efficiency in design practices.

Working in large enterprises as a UX designer requires a unique set of skills and strategies. UX designers must balance the needs of the organization, stakeholders, and users while navigating complex organizational structures and legacy systems. By building relationships with key decision-makers, advocating for UX best practices, leveraging user data and analytics, collaborating with cross-functional teams, and streamlining workflows, UX designers can achieve success in large enterprises.

The Global UX Puzzle: Strategies for Bridging Cultural Divides in Design

Designing user experiences for global companies is like trying to navigate through a foreign city without a map or a GPS. UX designers must deal with language barriers, cultural differences, and varying accessibility standards to create products and services that resonate with local users. In this chapter, we will explore strategies for UX designers working in global companies to overcome the localization challenge and deliver successful user experiences that don't get lost in translation.

Advantages

- Working in global companies means access to a diverse pool of talent, including local teams with knowledge of the market and culture. These insights can be invaluable in creating user experiences that feel local and familiar.
- Designing for a global audience means opportunities to broaden the impact of products and services beyond borders. It's like building a bridge that connects people from different parts of the world.
- Exposure to a wide range of languages, cultures, and accessibility standards can enrich the design process and lead to new insights and ideas that would not be possible otherwise.

Disadvantages

- Designing for diverse cultures, languages, and markets is like playing a game of cultural whack-a-mole. Adapting the user experience to local preferences, customs, and accessibility standards can be challenging and time-consuming.
- Localization efforts may require significant resources, including dedi-

cated teams, technology, and expertise. It's like building a tower of babel with the right tools and resources.

- Without a solid localization strategy, the user experience can be lost in translation. It's like sending a postcard in a foreign language that no one can read.

Tips for Designers

- **Conduct thorough user research in local markets:** UX designers should prioritize user research in local markets to gain insight into user needs, preferences, and behaviors. This research can inform design decisions and ensure that the user experience is tailored to local users.
- **Partner with local teams:** Working with local teams can be beneficial in understanding local markets, culture, and language. UX designers should collaborate with local teams to ensure that design decisions are aligned with local preferences and customs.
- **Leverage localization tools and best practices:** There are many localization tools and best practices available to UX designers. These tools can help streamline the localization process and ensure consistency in design and user experience across different languages and markets.
- **Design for accessibility:** Accessibility standards can vary significantly across different countries and regions. UX designers should design for accessibility from the outset and ensure that the user experience is accessible to all users, regardless of their location or language.

Designing for global companies presents unique challenges for UX designers. To overcome these challenges, UX designers should prioritize user research in local markets, partner with local teams, leverage localization tools and best practices, and design for accessibility. By taking these steps, UX designers can create successful user experiences that resonate with local users and contribute to the overall success of global companies.

The Chameleon Approach in Consulting or Agency Settings

Working as a UX designer in a consulting or agency setting can be a chameleon-like experience. UX designers must be adaptable and flexible to meet the needs of different clients, industries, and project requirements. In this chapter, we will explore strategies for UX designers in consulting or agency settings to succeed.

Advantages

- Opportunities to work on a variety of projects with diverse clients and industries, which can lead to professional growth and skill development.
- Exposure to different business models, workflows, and design methodologies, which can broaden one's perspective and expertise.
- Potential for high-impact work that can make a significant difference to clients and their users.

Disadvantages

- Clients may have varying levels of knowledge and understanding of UX design, which can lead to misaligned expectations and communication challenges.
- Projects may have tight timelines and budgets, which can make it difficult to deliver quality work and meet user needs.
- The need to constantly adapt to new clients, industries, and project requirements can lead to burnout and lack of consistency in design practices.

Tips for Designers

- **Be adaptable and flexible:** UX designers in consulting or agency settings must be willing to adapt to different clients, industries, and project requirements. This requires a flexible mindset and a willingness to learn new skills and methodologies.
- **Understand the client's business goals and user needs:** It is crucial to understand the client's business goals and user needs to deliver tailored solutions that meet their needs. This requires close collaboration with clients and a deep understanding of their business context and user personas.
- **Collaborate closely with clients:** Close collaboration with clients is key to success in consulting or agency settings. This requires effective communication, active listening, and the ability to build rapport with clients.
- **Leverage existing design systems or frameworks:** In consulting or agency settings, time and budget constraints can make it challenging to deliver quality work. UX designers can streamline workflows by leveraging existing design systems or frameworks to ensure consistency and efficiency in design practices.
- **Focus on delivering value:** In consulting or agency settings, it is important to focus on delivering value to clients and their users. This

requires a deep understanding of the client's business context and user needs, as well as a focus on delivering tangible results that meet their goals.

Working as a UX designer in a consulting or agency setting requires a chameleon-like approach. UX designers must be adaptable, flexible, and willing to learn new skills and methodologies to meet the needs of different clients, industries, and project requirements. By understanding the client's business goals and user needs, collaborating closely with clients, leveraging existing design systems or frameworks, and focusing on delivering value, UX designers can succeed in consulting or agency settings.

* * *

Chapter 12: UX Across the Board

Designers are the unsung heroes of the digital world, responsible for making sure our interactions with products and services are smooth and frustration-free. But, as with any hero, their job is not without its challenges, especially when it comes to dealing with the quirks of different industries. In this chapter, we'll explore the wild and wacky world of UX design across various industries, from the fast-paced world of tech to the stuffy halls of finance, and everything in between.

- **Healthcare:** UX designers in healthcare face the challenge of designing for a diverse range of users, including patients, healthcare providers, and administrative staff. The advantages of working in healthcare include the opportunity to make a positive impact on people's lives and access to cutting-edge technologies.

- **Education:** In the education industry, UX designers may need to design for students, teachers, and administrators. The advantages of working in education include the opportunity to shape the future of learning and the availability of a wealth of research on effective educational practices.
- **Finance:** UX designers in the finance industry face the challenge of designing for a wide range of users with different financial literacy levels and goals. The advantages of working in finance include the availability of data and resources to inform design decisions and the opportunity to create products that can have a significant impact on users' financial well-being.
- **Retail:** UX designers in the retail industry must design for both in-store and online experiences, often with a focus on increasing conversions and sales. The advantages of working in retail include the opportunity to innovate in a highly competitive industry and the availability of customer data to inform design decisions.
- **Travel and Hospitality:** UX designers in the travel and hospitality industry must design for a wide range of users, including tourists, business travelers, and hospitality staff. The advantages of working in travel and hospitality include the opportunity to create memorable experiences for users and access to emerging technologies such as virtual and augmented reality.
- **Technology:** In the technology industry, UX designers must design for a wide range of products and services, from mobile apps to enterprise software. The advantages of working in technology include the opportunity to work on cutting-edge products and services and access to resources such as user data and advanced analytics tools.
- **Automotive:** UX designers in the automotive industry must design for the driver, passengers, and the vehicle itself. The advantages of working in the automotive industry include the opportunity to shape the future of transportation and access to emerging technologies such as self-driving cars.

- **Gaming:** In the gaming industry, UX designers must design for a wide range of players, from casual gamers to hardcore enthusiasts. The advantages of working in gaming include the opportunity to innovate in a rapidly growing industry and access to emerging technologies such as virtual and augmented reality.
- **Non-profit:** UX designers in the non-profit sector must design for a variety of users, from volunteers to donors to those who benefit from the organization's services. The advantages of working in a non-profit include the opportunity to create products and services that can have a positive impact on society and contribute to a worthy cause.
- **Media and Entertainment:** UX designers in the media and entertainment industry must design for a wide range of users, from casual viewers to devoted fans. The advantages of working in media and entertainment include the opportunity to create engaging, immersive experiences that captivate and retain users.

In the coming sections, we will take a deep dive into some of the most prominent industries where UX design plays a critical role. We will explore the specific challenges and opportunities that UX designers face in each industry. By gaining a deeper understanding of these industries and their users, UX designers can create designs that are tailored to their specific needs, leading to improved user satisfaction and business success.

Paging Dr. UX: How Designers Are Reshaping the Future of Healthcare.

UX design isn't just for making fancy websites or apps that help you order pizza with one click. In the healthcare industry, UX designers play a crucial role in making sure that digital tools and services are accessible, easy to use, and most importantly, help people stay healthy. Let's take a look at what's going on in healthcare UX design and why it's an exciting field to be in.

The State of Healthcare UX Design

If you think healthcare is still stuck in the Stone Age, think again. In recent years, healthcare has seen a massive push towards digital transformation. Telemedicine, electronic medical records, and other healthcare applications are all examples of the growing need for UX design in the healthcare industry.

Telemedicine has become increasingly popular, especially after the pandemic made in-person visits a risky business. With telemedicine, patients can connect with their doctors from the comfort of their own homes. However, if the user experience of the telemedicine application is subpar, patients may encounter difficulties in accessing and using the platform, leading to frustration and potential health risks. For example, if the app is confusing or difficult to navigate, patients may struggle to schedule appointments or find important information, which could lead to missed appointments or delayed treatment. That's where UX designers come in – they play a crucial role in ensuring that telemedicine applications are designed in a way that is user-friendly, intuitive, and accessible to all patients.

Electronic medical records (EMRs) are another area where UX design is critical. These digital versions of patient records allow healthcare providers to keep track of patient health information, but if the design is confusing, it can cause serious problems. UX designers need to make sure that EMRs are easy to navigate, user-friendly, and accessible to healthcare providers.

Challenges in Healthcare UX Design

Designing for healthcare comes with unique challenges. One of the most significant challenges is ensuring that digital tools and services comply with strict regulations and standards like HIPAA and GDPR. UX designers need to make sure that patient privacy and security are never compromised.

Another challenge is designing for accessibility. Healthcare applications must be designed to meet the needs of all patients, including those with disabilities. UX designers need to ensure that applications are easy to use for everyone, regardless of their abilities.

Why Healthcare UX Design is Exciting

Solving healthcare problems requires empathy, creativity, and a deep understanding of user needs. By working with healthcare professionals, patients, and other stakeholders, UX designers can have a significant impact on society. The potential benefits of UX design in healthcare are vast, from improving patient outcomes to reducing healthcare costs and increasing patient satisfaction.

In healthcare, UX design is not just about creating pretty interfaces. It's about designing tools and services that can help people live healthier lives. And that's what makes healthcare UX design an exciting field to be in.

UX design is a critical component of the healthcare industry's push towards digital transformation. Telemedicine, electronic medical records, and other healthcare applications require UX designers to make sure they are accessible, easy to use, and secure. While there are unique challenges in healthcare UX design, the potential impact on society makes it an exciting field to be in. By creating digital tools and services that are user-friendly and efficient, UX designers can make a real difference in the lives of patients and healthcare professionals.

From ABC to UX: Navigating the Wild World of Educational Design

The education industry presents unique challenges and opportunities for UX designers. In this chapter, we will explore the advantages of working in education and the challenges UX designers face when designing for students, teachers, and administrators.

Advantages of Working in Education

UX designers in the education industry have the opportunity to shape the future of learning. They can work with teachers and administrators to design tools that make learning more effective, engaging, and accessible to all students. The education industry also provides a wealth of research on effective educational practices that UX designers can use to inform their work.

Designing for students in the education industry can be particularly rewarding. UX designers can create interfaces that support the diverse needs of students, such as those with learning disabilities or limited English proficiency. By designing interfaces that are inclusive and accessible, UX designers can help ensure that all students have the opportunity to learn and succeed.

Challenges in Education UX Design

The education industry is complex, with multiple stakeholders involved in the learning process, including students, teachers, and administrators. UX designers must consider the needs of each group when designing educational tools. For example, a tool designed for students may need to be adapted for use by teachers or administrators.

Another challenge is the limited budget often allocated to educational technology. UX designers may need to be creative in finding ways to implement best practices with limited resources. Additionally, the education industry is highly regulated, with strict requirements for data privacy and security. UX designers must ensure that their designs comply with these regulations.

Why it is Interesting for UX Designers to Solve Problems in Education

Solving problems in education presents a unique opportunity for UX designers to make a positive impact on society. By designing tools that support effective learning, UX designers can help ensure that students have the skills and knowledge they need to succeed in the future. Moreover, education technology is a rapidly growing field, providing a wealth of opportunities for UX designers to develop innovative solutions.

Solving problems in education requires collaboration with teachers, administrators, and students. UX designers can work with these stakeholders to gain a deep understanding of their needs and create interfaces that meet those needs. By doing so, UX designers can help improve the learning experience for all students.

UX design plays a critical role in the education industry. Despite the challenges of designing for multiple stakeholders and limited budgets, UX designers have the opportunity to shape the future of learning. By designing tools that are inclusive, accessible, and effective, UX designers can help ensure that all students have the opportunity to learn and succeed. Solving problems in education is a unique and rewarding challenge that UX designers should embrace.

UX Design in Finance

Money doesn't grow on trees, but it certainly grows on FinTech startups. With the rise of digital banking, UX designers in the finance industry have their work cut out for them. But hey, at least they don't have to deal with the hassle of standing in line at the bank anymore.

Mobile banking apps have made it easier than ever to manage your finances on the go. You can even check your bank balance while waiting in line at the coffee shop. Just make sure you don't accidentally transfer all your funds to the barista.

Investment platforms are like Tinder for stocks. Swipe left if you don't like the company's financials, swipe right if you think they're a good investment.

Challenges in UX Design in Finance

One challenge in UX design in finance is making sure that financial applications are compliant with regulations like **GDPR** and **PSD2**. It's like walking a tightrope between designing a user-friendly interface and making sure you don't accidentally leak people's financial information. It's a good thing UX designers have a keen eye for detail.

GDPR (General Data Protection Regulation) is a set of rules created by the European Union (EU) to protect people's personal information. It gives individuals more control over their data and how it's used by companies. For example, companies must ask for permission before collecting someone's data and must keep it safe from unauthorized access.

PSD2 (Payment Services Directive 2) is a regulation also created by the European Union (EU) that focuses on online payments. It requires banks and other payment providers to make it easier and safer for people to use online payment services. It also promotes competition by allowing people to use third-party payment providers to manage their online payments.

Both GDPR and PSD2 aim to protect people's privacy and personal information while promoting safer and more secure online experiences.

Another challenge is designing financial applications that are accessible to all users, including those with limited financial literacy. It's like trying to explain the stock market to your grandma. You need to keep it simple and use a lot of analogies. "Think of the stock market like a giant yard sale, Grandma. Sometimes you find a treasure, sometimes you get ripped off."

Why Finance UX Design is Exciting

UX design isn't just about creating visually appealing interfaces; it's about making money work for people and not the other way around. The finance industry is constantly evolving, and UX designers are in high demand to help solve problems in this area. Understanding user needs and using creativity and empathy are essential to designing financial applications that won't make users want to pull their hair out!

But designing financial applications isn't just about making people's lives easier; it's about improving financial literacy, helping users achieve their goals, and even changing society. Who knows, your work as a UX designer in the finance industry could be the next big thing that convinces your parents you made the right career choice!

UX design is a vital and exciting career in the finance industry. Challenges such as regulatory compliance and accessibility exist, but the potential to make a real difference in the lives of users makes it an exhilarating area for UX designers to solve problems. So let's design some financial applications that are not only user-friendly, accessible, and secure but also put the "fun" back in "funds"!

From Shopping Carts to Customer Hearts: The Fun World of Retail UX Design

Welcome to the world of Retail UX Design, where we believe that a good design can turn window shoppers into regular customers! As a Retail UX Designer, you have the power to create immersive experiences both in-store and online that make users go "Wow" and "Take my money!"

The Challenges of Retail UX Design

One of the biggest challenges in Retail UX Design is finding the right balance between business goals and user needs. After all, the primary objective of most retail companies is to make sales and increase conversions. However, this cannot be achieved at the expense of the user experience. The key is to find creative solutions that satisfy both the business and user needs.

Another challenge is the fast-paced nature of the retail industry. Trends and customer preferences change quickly, and it's crucial to stay ahead of the game. Retail UX Designers must be agile and adaptable, always willing to experiment with new ideas and iterate quickly.

The Advantages of Retail UX Design

The retail industry is one of the most competitive and constantly evolving industries out there, and as a Retail UX Designer, you have the opportunity to innovate and create experiences that stand out from the crowd. With access to vast amounts of customer data, you can make informed design decisions that drive conversions and sales.

Moreover, Retail UX Designers have the opportunity to work on a wide range of projects, from designing immersive in-store experiences to crafting seamless online shopping experiences. The possibilities are endless, and your designs have the potential to impact millions of customers worldwide.

Retail UX Design is a dynamic and exciting field that offers a unique set of challenges and advantages. As a Retail UX Designer, you have the power to create experiences that are both visually appealing and highly functional. By finding the right balance between business goals and user needs, you can help companies increase conversions, build brand loyalty, and create experiences that customers will never forget. So, what are you waiting for? Let's get designing!

Buckle Up, Travelers: The Thrilling World of Travel and Hospitality UX Design

Welcome to the world of Travel and Hospitality UX Design, where the journey is just as important as the destination! As a Travel and Hospitality UX Designer, you have the power to create unforgettable experiences for tourists, business travelers, and hospitality staff.

The Challenges of Travel and Hospitality UX Design

One of the biggest challenges in Travel and Hospitality UX Design is designing for a diverse range of users with varying needs and preferences. Tourists may be looking for immersive experiences that showcase the local culture, while business travelers may prioritize efficiency and convenience. Meanwhile, hospitality staff may require user-friendly tools that help them manage their workload.

Another challenge is the complexity of travel and hospitality systems, which can be difficult to navigate for users. It's crucial to design interfaces that are intuitive and user-friendly, while also providing all the necessary information and features.

The Advantages of Travel and Hospitality UX Design

The travel and hospitality industry is constantly evolving, with new technologies and trends emerging all the time. As a Travel and Hospitality UX Designer, you have the opportunity to work on cutting-edge projects that incorporate emerging technologies such as virtual and augmented reality.

Moreover, you have the chance to create memorable experiences for millions of users worldwide. Whether it's designing a user-friendly booking platform or crafting an immersive in-flight entertainment system, your designs have the potential to impact the way people experience travel and hospitality.

Travel and Hospitality UX Design is an exciting and rewarding field that offers a unique set of challenges and opportunities. As a Travel and Hospitality UX Designer, you have the power to create experiences that are both functional and memorable, whether it's for tourists, business travelers, or hospitality staff. By designing interfaces that are intuitive, user-friendly, and visually appealing, you can help users navigate complex systems and enjoy the journey just as much as the destination. So, pack your bags, and let's design some unforgettable experiences!

UX in Technology: From Buzzword to Game Changer

Welcome to the fantastical world of UX design in the tech industry, where your creativity knows no bounds and the speed is faster than a cheetah on a caffeine rush! As a UX designer in the tech industry, you get to wield your magic wand to shape the future of digital products and services, from life-changing mobile apps to enterprise software that'll make your head spin.

The Challenges of UX Design in Technology

One of the biggest challenges in UX design in the technology industry is the need to constantly innovate and stay ahead of the competition. With new technologies and platforms emerging every day, it can be difficult to maintain consistency in design and user experience across products and services.

Moreover, some technology companies may not have a deep understanding or appreciation for the value of UX design. As a UX designer, you may need to educate and convince leadership about the benefits of a user-centered approach, rather than simply making cosmetic changes to existing products.

The Advantages of UX Design in Technology

As a UX designer in a technology company, you could be working on really cutting-edge tech, like drones! Drones are revolutionizing industries such as aerial photography, mapping, delivery, and agriculture, among others. Your role as a UX designer could involve designing intuitive and user-friendly interfaces for drone control systems, creating seamless experiences for aerial data capture and analysis, and optimizing user interactions with drones through mobile apps or web interfaces.

The fast-paced nature of the technology industry means that as a UX designer, you'll constantly be at the forefront of innovation, designing for new platforms, devices, and interfaces that push the boundaries of what's possible. You'll have the opportunity to work with cross-functional teams, including engineers, product managers, and data scientists, to create compelling user experiences that harness the full potential of cutting-edge technology.

In addition, the technology industry is characterized by rapid changes and evolving user needs, requiring UX designers to constantly adapt and iterate their designs. You may be involved in user research, usability testing, and data-driven design iterations to continuously improve the user experience of your products and services.

Working in a technology company as a UX designer can be an exciting and fulfilling experience, where you have the chance to contribute to the development of groundbreaking products and services that shape the way people interact with technology. It's a unique opportunity to combine your creative skills with the latest technological advancements, and make a meaningful impact on the world of user experience.

Revving Up User Experience: The Awesome World of Automotive UX Design

Welcome to the world of automotive UX design, where driving experiences go beyond just getting from point A to point B. As a UX designer in this industry, you have the power to create experiences that delight and enhance the safety and efficiency of drivers and passengers alike.

User-Centered Design: Putting the Driver First

One of the most significant trends in automotive UX design is user-centered design. In this approach, the driver is placed at the center of the design process, and all design decisions are made with their needs and preferences in mind. This trend has been fueled by advances in technology, such as voice-activated assistants and machine learning algorithms, which make it possible to create more personalized experiences for drivers.

Connected Cars: Enhancing the Driving Experience

Another emerging trend is connected cars, which are vehicles that are equipped with internet connectivity and other advanced technologies. Connected cars can offer a wide range of benefits, such as real-time traffic updates, remote vehicle control, and enhanced safety features. Automotive UX designers must consider how to design interfaces that allow drivers to interact with these features in a safe and intuitive way.

Autonomous Driving: Redefining the Driving Experience

Perhaps the most significant trend in automotive UX design is the emergence of autonomous driving technology. Self-driving cars have the potential to revolutionize the way we think about transportation, from reducing traffic congestion to improving road safety. As autonomous driving technology becomes more advanced, automotive UX designers must consider how to design interfaces that allow drivers to interact with the car in a seamless and intuitive way.

The Challenges of Automotive UX Design

One of the biggest challenges of automotive UX design is finding the right balance between entertainment and safety. Drivers and passengers want to be connected and entertained while on the road, but it's crucial to prioritize safety features such as intuitive controls and clear displays that don't distract from driving. Achieving this balance requires a deep understanding of user behavior and the ability to create designs that enhance the driving experience.

Another challenge is keeping up with the rapid pace of the automotive industry. With constantly evolving technology, automotive UX designers must stay ahead of the game by researching new features and anticipating customer needs. They must be willing to take risks and innovate to keep up with the competition.

The Advantages of Automotive UX Design

Working in automotive UX design provides the unique opportunity to shape the future of transportation. UX designers can create experiences that have a significant impact on people's lives, whether they're driving to work or embarking on a cross-country road trip.

Furthermore, the industry is constantly evolving with the introduction of self-driving cars, connected vehicles, and electric cars. Automotive UX designers can work on cutting-edge projects that push the boundaries of what's possible and make transportation safer and more efficient for all.

The Exciting World of Gaming UX Design

Welcome to the exciting, fast-paced world of gaming UX design! As a designer in this industry, you have the power to create immersive and engaging experiences that keep players coming back for more. However, with great power comes great responsibility, and there are some unique challenges that you'll face in this field.

The Challenges of Gaming UX Design

One of the biggest challenges in gaming UX design is balancing business goals with user needs. Many game publishers and designers are more interested in making money than providing a great user experience, and they may sneak in full-page ads or force users to buy add-ons to increase revenue. It can be frustrating as a designer to try to maintain a balance between making a profit and providing a fun, enjoyable experience for players.

Another challenge is the potential for addiction, especially in games that use gambling-like mechanics. As designers, we need to be aware of the potential harm that these mechanics can cause and take steps to ensure that our games are not promoting addictive behaviors.

On top of these challenges, there are often tight deadlines in the gaming industry. This can be stressful, but it also provides an opportunity to think creatively and come up with innovative solutions to problems on the fly.

The Advantages of Gaming UX Design

The world of gaming UX design is not only filled with challenges, but it also offers unique advantages that make it an exciting and fun industry to work in. One of the major perks is the opportunity to explore different types of games and create experiences that are engaging and immersive. From casual mobile games to AAA console titles, as a gaming UX designer, you have the chance to work on a wide variety of projects and unleash your creativity in different genres and platforms.

Another advantage is that gaming UX designers often have the opportunity to play games at work! It's not just about designing user experiences, but also experiencing the games firsthand to understand how they work and how players interact with them. This allows designers to have a deeper understanding of the gaming landscape and create designs that are tailored to the needs and preferences of the players.

Additionally, the gaming industry is known for its vibrant and dynamic culture, with a passionate community of gamers and developers. This creates a stimulating environment for designers to collaborate, exchange ideas, and continuously learn and improve their skills. The fast-paced nature of the industry also means that there are always new trends, technologies, and design approaches to explore, keeping designers on their toes and pushing them to stay innovative and up-to-date.

Gaming UX design is a challenging yet exciting field with unique challenges and opportunities. As designers, we need to be aware of the potential for addiction and balance business goals with user needs. But with hard work and creativity, we can create experiences that keep players engaged and coming back for more. So, let's level up and make some awesome games!

Designing for Good: The Role of UX Design in the Non-Profit Sector

UX designers in the non-profit sector play a critical role in creating products and services that have a positive impact on society. From designing websites that facilitate donations to creating apps that connect volunteers with opportunities, UX designers in this industry must design for a wide range of users with diverse needs and goals.

Challenges in Non-Profit UX Design

One of the biggest challenges in non-profit UX design is navigating limited budgets and resources. Non-profit organizations often operate on shoestring budgets, which can limit the scope of design projects and make it challenging to invest in user research and testing.

Another challenge is designing for accessibility and inclusivity. Non-profit organizations often serve marginalized communities, which means UX designers must prioritize accessibility features such as screen reader compatibility and color contrast. Additionally, designing for inclusivity requires understanding the needs and goals of diverse stakeholders, such as volunteers, donors, and those who benefit from the organization's services.

Finally, incorporating feedback from diverse stakeholders can be challenging in the non-profit sector. Organizations may have multiple stakeholders with different priorities and goals, and UX designers must navigate these conflicting perspectives while maintaining a user-centric approach.

Advantages of Non-Profit UX Design

Despite these challenges, UX designers in the non-profit sector have the opportunity to create products and services that have a meaningful impact on society. Designing for a worthy cause can be personally rewarding, and it allows designers to use their skills to contribute to something larger than themselves.

Additionally, non-profit organizations often have a strong sense of mission and purpose, which can help UX designers prioritize user needs and design for positive outcomes. Finally, the non-profit sector is a growing industry that is increasingly recognizing the value of user-centered design, providing ample opportunities for UX designers to innovate and make a difference.

UX designers in the non-profit sector play a vital role in creating products and services that serve the needs of diverse stakeholders and contribute to a worthy cause. While challenges such as limited budgets and resources, designing for accessibility and inclusivity, and incorporating feedback from diverse stakeholders can be daunting, the rewards of designing for good are immeasurable. UX designers in this industry have the opportunity to make a real difference in the world, and their work can have a lasting impact on society.

UX Designers, Lights, Camera, Action! The Adventures of Media and Entertainment UX

Welcome to the world of media and entertainment UX, where designers have the power to take users on an unforgettable ride. From binge-watchers to super-fans, UX designers in this industry must cater to a diverse audience and always keep it fresh to keep up with ever-changing trends.

Let's dive into the unique challenges and perks of working in media and entertainment UX design. Brace yourselves, folks!

The Challenges of Media and Entertainment UX Design

One of the challenges of media and entertainment UX design is working within tight deadlines and limited budgets. Designers are often required to deliver high-quality designs quickly, requiring them to work efficiently and creatively within the constraints they have.

Another challenge is creating designs for an audience that's more unpredictable than the weather. Trends in media and entertainment can shift in a heartbeat, and designers have to be ready to create experiences that appeal to everyone. Finally, media and entertainment UX designers have to deal with sneaky companies trying to slip full-page ads and push unwanted add-ons

The Advantages of Media and Entertainment UX Design

One of the biggest perks of working in media and entertainment UX is the chance to create immersive experiences that suck users in. UX designers can work on anything from traditional media like TV and film to cutting-edge tech like VR and AR.

Furthermore, designers have the opportunity to influence pop culture and create experiences that will be remembered for ages. Imagine being the one to create the next cultural phenomenon that everybody talks about.

The industry is always evolving, offering UX designers a chance to stay ahead of the game and work with the latest technology.

Media and entertainment UX design is a wild and exhilarating field that has its own share of challenges and perks. UX designers can create unforgettable experiences that leave users craving more while dealing with tight deadlines, ever-changing trends, and sneaky companies. By staying ahead of the game, designing for a diverse audience, and prioritizing user safety, designers can create experiences that make a lasting impact on pop culture. So, let's dive into the world of media and entertainment UX and create experiences that take users on a journey they'll never forget!

As a UX designer, it's important to choose an industry that you're passionate about. This is because you'll be working on industry-specific projects and it's essential that you enjoy your work. Whether it's healthcare, finance, or e-commerce, each industry has its own unique challenges and opportunities for UX design.

To create good UX design, you must have a deep understanding of the user, their needs, and their pain points. Collaboration and communication with team members are key. You should also be flexible and adaptable because projects and industries can change rapidly.

Ultimately, a successful UX designer is someone who is passionate about problem-solving, willing to learn and adapt, and has a good understanding of their industry's specific needs and challenges. By creating experiences that are both usable and enjoyable for users, UX designers can drive business success and improve people's lives.

* * *

Chapter 13: Decoding UX Team Structures

When it comes to searching for a job as a UX designer, it's crucial to have an understanding of UX team structure to ensure a positive work experience. The success of a project is heavily reliant on the effectiveness of the UX team, making it vital to comprehend the different structures that may be encountered and what each entails.

Building a successful UX team can be compared to laying the groundwork for a house. The right team structure provides a solid foundation for a project's success. As a UX designer, it's imperative to understand team structures and choose the appropriate one to have a successful and rewarding career in UX design.

There is no one-size-fits-all approach to team organization for UX teams. Different companies may structure their teams differently, driven by the size of the company, the industry, the nature of the project, or other factors.

Here are three common types of team organization for UX teams:

- **The UX Hub:** This structure revolves around a central UX team, with all design, research, and development work funneled through them. This team has the authority to make decisions and set design standards across the organization. While this structure provides a clear sense of direction and consistency, it can also lead to bottlenecks and a lack of innovation outside of the core team.
- **The Agile Squad:** In this structure, cross-functional teams are formed for each project, consisting of a mix of designers, developers, and other specialists. These teams work in short sprints, collaborating closely and iterating quickly to deliver high-quality results. While this structure allows for flexibility and fast iteration, it can be challenging to coordinate and maintain consistency across multiple teams.
- **The Embedded Team:** With this structure, UX designers are embedded within different product or project teams, working alongside developers and other stakeholders to ensure a seamless integration of UX design. This structure allows for close collaboration and alignment with specific goals, but may lead to a lack of standardization across different products or projects.

Each of these team structures has its strengths and weaknesses, and the right choice will depend on the specific needs and circumstances of the project. It's important to consider factors such as the size of the team, the complexity of the project, the level of collaboration required, and the budget available when choosing a team organization structure. In the following sections, we will explore each of these team structures in more detail, looking at the benefits and challenges of each and offering practical tips on how to build and manage successful UX teams.

Building a Consistent User Experience: Exploring the UX Hub Organizational Structure

The **UX Hub** organizational structure is a common approach used in organizations where the user experience is a critical component of their product or service. This structure revolves around a central UX team that acts as a hub for all design, research, and front-end or UI development work. The team has the authority to make decisions and set design standards across the organization.

The **UX Hub** structure provides a clear sense of direction and consistency, which can be beneficial for organizations that require a standardized approach to their user experience. By having a centralized team responsible for the user experience, organizations can ensure that all products and services meet a consistent level of quality. This can help build trust and loyalty among customers, who know they can expect a consistent experience regardless of the product or service they are using.

However, the **UX Hub** structure can also lead to bottlenecks and a lack of innovation outside of the core team. Because all design, research, and development work must go through the central UX team, other teams may feel stifled in their ability to innovate and experiment with new ideas. This can result in a lack of creativity and a slower pace of innovation, which can be detrimental to an organization's ability to remain competitive in their market.

To address this challenge, organizations with a **UX Hub** structure can implement strategies to encourage innovation and collaboration outside of the central team. For example, they can establish cross-functional teams that include members from different departments to work on specific projects. This approach allows for greater collaboration and idea sharing, which can lead to more innovative solutions.

Another strategy is to establish a culture of experimentation and continuous improvement across the organization. By encouraging all employees to be involved in the user experience process, organizations can foster a culture of innovation and creativity. This can lead to a more dynamic and responsive organization that can quickly adapt to changing market conditions.

Flexible, Fast, and Effective: An In-Depth Look at the Agile Squad Organizational Structure

The **Agile Squad** organizational structure is a popular approach used in organizations where agility and flexibility are essential for success. In this structure, cross-functional teams are formed for each project, consisting of a mix of designers, developers, and other specialists. These teams work in short sprints, collaborating closely and iterating quickly to deliver high-quality results.

One of the main benefits of the **Agile Squad** approach is its flexibility. Because each team is assembled specifically for a project, it can adapt to changing requirements and priorities. This allows organizations to quickly pivot and respond to changes in the market or user needs. Additionally, the **Agile Squad** approach promotes a culture of collaboration, with team members working closely together to achieve shared goals. This can help build trust and camaraderie among team members and foster a sense of ownership and accountability for the success of the project.

However, the **Agile Squad** approach can also present challenges, particularly in terms of coordination and consistency. With multiple teams working on different projects simultaneously, it can be difficult to maintain consistent design and development standards across the organization. This can lead to inconsistencies in the user experience, which can negatively impact customer trust and loyalty.

To address these challenges, organizations using the **Agile Squad** approach can implement strategies to promote consistency and coordination across teams. For example, they can establish design and development guidelines to ensure that all teams are adhering to a consistent set of standards. They can also establish regular cross-functional team reviews to ensure that teams are aligned and working towards shared goals.

Another strategy is to invest in tools and technologies that facilitate collaboration and communication across teams. By providing teams with shared spaces for collaboration and information sharing, such as project management software or digital design systems, organizations can help promote consistency and coordination across teams.

The Power of In-Team Collaboration: An Exploration of the Embedded Team Model

Embedded design teams are a type of design team that is composed of designers who are embedded within different product or project teams. These teams usually consist of cross-functional members from different departments, such as engineering, product management, and design.

One of the benefits of this approach is that designers can have a deep understanding of the project and work closely with other members of the product development team. Being embedded within a project team allows designers to get involved in the early stages of product development, which can help ensure that the final product meets user needs and is aligned with the overall project vision.

In addition, designers can build relationships with other members of the team, such as engineers and product managers. Building relationships with colleagues from different areas can help designers to better understand project constraints and requirements, and can help to facilitate more productive discussions about design solutions.

However, there are also potential downsides to this approach. One of the main challenges of **embedded design teams** is that there may be a lack of standardization across different products or projects. Because designers are embedded within different teams, there may be inconsistencies in terms of design and development practices. This can lead to inconsistencies in the user experience across different products or projects, which can negatively impact customer trust and loyalty.

To address these challenges, organizations using the **embedded team** approach can implement strategies to promote consistency and standardization across different products or projects. One such strategy is to establish design and development guidelines to ensure that all teams are adhering to a consistent set of standards. Another strategy is to invest in tools and technologies that facilitate collaboration and information sharing across different teams, such as digital design systems or centralized repositories for design assets.

Another potential challenge of **embedded design teams** is that designers may feel isolated from their peers. Because there is often only one designer working on a project, it can be difficult to collaborate with other designers or receive feedback on design decisions. This can lead to designers feeling isolated or disconnected from the broader design community.

To address this challenge, organizations can implement strategies to facilitate collaboration and knowledge sharing among designers. One such strategy is to pair designers together on projects, which can help to build trust and support between designers. Another strategy is to provide designers with opportunities to participate in design communities or professional development programs, which can help them to stay connected to the broader design community.

Design teams can come in many shapes and sizes. As a beginner designer, it can be intimidating to enter into different types of design teams, each with its own quirks and idiosyncrasies. But fear not, intrepid designer! We've got you covered with some tips for working in each type of team:

- **The UX Hub:** Welcome to the mothership, cadet! In this type of team, you'll be surrounded by other designers who share your passion for typography and color theory. On the plus side, you'll always have someone to nerd out with. On the downside, you might start to forget what the outside world looks like. To keep yourself grounded, make sure to connect with other departments and get a sense of how your work fits into the bigger picture.

- **The Agile Squad:** Get ready to sprint, champ! In this type of team, you'll be working closely with designers, developers, and other specialists to deliver high-quality results in short bursts. On the plus side, you'll be able to iterate quickly and have lots of opportunities for collaboration. On the downside, it can be tough to keep track of who's doing what, so make sure to establish clear roles and communication channels from the get-go.

- **The Embedded Team:** You're in this for the long haul, partner! In this type of team, you'll be working alongside product managers, developers, and other stakeholders to ensure a seamless integration of UX design. On the plus side, you'll have deep knowledge of the project and be able to work closely with other team members. On the downside, you might start to feel like you're the only designer in the world. To combat isolation, make sure to connect with other designers outside of your team and attend design events.

No matter what type of team you find yourself in, remember to stay curious, ask questions, and be open to new perspectives. And of course, always keep a healthy supply of snacks on hand – you never know when you might need to bribe a developer!

* * *

Chapter 14: Talking About Your Work

Crafting effective UX designs isn't just about making decisions out of thin air. As a UX designer, it's essential to have research and data to support your choices, similar to a detective gathering clues to solve a user's needs and goals. It's not about personal preferences but rather presenting concrete evidence to support your design decisions and persuade stakeholders. Think of it as making your case with the evidence in the court of stakeholder opinions.

When it comes to presenting your UX design, imagine yourself as a lawyer in a courtroom drama. Your research and data are your compelling evidence, and you need to be prepared to present multiple design options and alternatives as exhibits to support your case. Be ready to counter objections with well-reasoned arguments, just like a skilled attorney cross-examining a witness. And just like in a courtroom, maintaining confidence and professionalism is crucial, as you plead your case for your meticulously crafted design.

But beware, there may be naysayers who think they know better, even if they lack a deep understanding of UX design. It's like having someone argue in court without knowing the difference between a gavel and a gavotte. So, be patient and explain the intricacies of UX design in simple terms, and perhaps even have them sketch their own solutions to give them a taste of the design process.

Remember, it's not just about presenting your design, but also being open to feedback and willing to consider different perspectives. It's similar to a dance, where you lead with your design, but also gracefully follow the rhythm of constructive criticism. It's a tango of creativity and collaboration, where your design and your ability to think critically are your dancing partners.

In the end, teamwork is essential. Involving as many team members as possible in the review process can help ensure that everyone is on the same page. Think of it as a brainstorming session where everyone gets to share their thoughts and opinions, and you're the facilitator, orchestrating the conversation and harmonizing the design direction. So, gather feedback, listen to the different beats, and remix your design accordingly.

So, to sum it up, presenting and defending your UX design is not for the faint-hearted. It requires the skills of a detective, the eloquence of a lawyer, and the flexibility of a dancer. Be armed with research and data, exude confidence and professionalism, and embrace collaboration and teamwork. With these tools in hand, you'll be ready to win the case for your UX design masterpiece! May the UX force be with you!

UXceptional Results: Unveiling the Value of User-Centric Design

As a UX designer, you possess a superpower - the ability to create exceptional user experiences that can optimize the entire product development process and save your business money by reducing rework. However, convincing leadership to prioritize UX may sometimes feel like an uphill battle. Here's how you can leverage your skills to make a compelling case:

Educate with Impactful Data: To persuade leaders of the importance of UX, it's important to present them with impactful data. One effective way to do this is to gather and present compelling data that demonstrates the tangible benefits of UX. For example, a well-designed user experience can result in higher conversion rates, increased customer retention, and improved business outcomes.

To make the case even stronger, highlight case studies and success stories from other companies to showcase the real impact of UX on the bottom line. By presenting this evidence, leaders can see firsthand the positive effects of UX and how it can contribute to their own company's success. It's also important to tailor the data to the specific needs and goals of the company. For example, if the company is focused on increasing sales, present data on how UX can improve conversion rates.

In addition to presenting data, it's important to educate leaders on the value of UX and why it should be prioritized in their company. By demonstrating the potential ROI of investing in UX, leaders can better understand why it's worth the time and resources. By working together with leaders and presenting them with compelling data, UX designers can help ensure that UX is given the attention and resources it deserves.

In 2018, IBM conducted a study on the ROI of design thinking. According to a Medium article published by IBM, they found that **for every $1 invested in design, companies could expect a return of $10-$100 in increased revenue**, reduced costs, and improved team efficiency.

IBM's study included a diverse range of companies, from startups to large enterprises, in industries such as healthcare, finance, and retail. They found that companies who used design thinking to inform their product development process saw significant improvements in customer satisfaction, employee engagement, and business performance.

Speak the Language of Business: When pitching UX to leadership, frame it in the context of business goals and objectives. Show how UX aligns with the company's vision and mission. Emphasize how investing in UX can lead to cost savings by reducing re-work, improving customer satisfaction, and boosting revenue. Use business metrics and key performance indicators (KPIs) to illustrate the value proposition of UX in terms that resonate with leadership.

Demonstrate User Empathy: Help leadership understand that putting users at the forefront is not just a nice-to-have, but a strategic imperative. Use your design skills to create user personas, customer journey maps, and usability reports that highlight pain points, challenges, and opportunities. Conduct user research and testing to uncover insights that show how addressing user needs and goals through UX can result in long-term customer loyalty and advocacy.

Show the Design Process: When working with leadership, it's important to show them the value of user-centric design and how it can benefit the business. One way to do this is by sharing your design process with them. This can help to demystify UX and show leadership the steps involved in creating a user-friendly product or service.

- First, start with your research phase. This involves understanding your users, their needs, and pain points. By showing leadership the insights you gather during this phase, you can highlight how UX can create solutions that address real user needs.
- Next, walk them through your wireframing and prototyping phases. Show how these steps can help to identify usability issues early on, before development even begins. This can save time and resources in the long run by avoiding costly design changes later on.
- Finally, showcase your testing phase. This is where you validate your design assumptions by testing your prototypes with real users. Share the insights and feedback you gather during this phase to highlight how UX can create a user-centric design that meets user needs and drives business results.

As an example, Airbnb showcases their design process through their design blog, Airbnb Design. They share insights into their research and testing methods, as well as design challenges they faced and how they overcame them. By sharing their process, Airbnb not only demystifies UX for their leadership, but also helps to build credibility and trust with their users.

Pilot and Iterate: If leadership is hesitant to fully commit to UX, suggest starting with a pilot project to demonstrate its value. Select a small project or feature and apply UX principles to design and test an improved user experience. Gather data and insights from the pilot to show the positive impact of UX on user satisfaction, engagement, and business outcomes. Use this evidence to advocate for broader integration of UX into the product development process.

Unleashing the Power of UX Design - Solving Problems and Innovating!

Imagine a world where every product or service is designed with the user at its core, where problems are identified and solved in innovative and delightful ways. Welcome to the world of UX design - a realm where creativity, empathy, and innovation intersect to create meaningful experiences for users.

UX design is often misunderstood as merely a step in the process of creating a visually appealing user interface (UI). However, it goes beyond aesthetics and is a strategic approach to problem-solving that encompasses the entire user experience. It's about understanding users, identifying their pain points, and designing solutions that address their needs in unique and innovative ways.

At its core, UX design is about **innovation**. It's about pushing the boundaries, thinking outside the box, and coming up with novel solutions to complex problems. It's about challenging the status quo and constantly striving to make things better for users. UX designers are the champions of innovation, constantly seeking ways to improve and enhance the user experience.

One of the key aspects of UX design is identifying problems and solving them in innovative ways. UX designers are like detectives, always on the lookout for pain points that users encounter in their journey. They conduct thorough research, gather insights, and analyze data to understand the root causes of these problems. They dig deep to uncover the underlying issues that users face and use their creativity and problem-solving skills to come up with innovative solutions.

But it's not just about fixing existing problems. UX designers also anticipate future problems and design with foresight. They think ahead and design solutions that can adapt to changing user needs and technological advancements. They envision possibilities and create experiences that are future-proof, ensuring that users' needs are met even as the landscape evolves.

UX design is not limited to a specific industry or domain. It applies to various contexts, from websites and mobile apps to physical products, services, and environments. It's about understanding the context in which users interact with a product or service and designing accordingly. It's about creating seamless and enjoyable experiences that delight users, regardless of the platform or medium.

Another crucial aspect of UX design is empathy. UX designers immerse themselves in the users' world, understanding their motivations, emotions, and behaviors. They put themselves in the users' shoes, seeing the world from their perspective. Empathy allows UX designers to design experiences that truly resonate with users, addressing their needs and desires in a meaningful way.

Innovation in UX design also involves thinking beyond the obvious. It's about finding unconventional solutions and challenging traditional approaches. It's about taking risks and being willing to fail in order to learn and improve. UX designers are not afraid to question the status quo and seek out new ways of doing things. They are the catalysts for change, driving innovation and pushing boundaries.

There have been several revolutionary innovations in the history of UX design that have transformed the industry and brought it to where it is today. Here are a few examples:

The graphical user interface (GUI) - This innovation changed the way people interacted with computers. Before the GUI, users had to type commands in a text-based interface. The GUI introduced icons, buttons, and other graphical elements that made it easier and more intuitive for users to navigate and interact with computer applications. The GUI was first popularized by Apple's Lisa computer in 1983 and later refined in the Macintosh in 1984.

Responsive web design - With the rise of smartphones and other mobile devices, designers had to rethink how they approached web design. Responsive web design emerged as a solution, allowing websites to adapt to different screen sizes and device types. Ethan Marcotte coined the term "responsive web design" in 2010, and it has since become a standard practice in web design.

Human-centered design - This approach puts the user at the center of the design process, emphasizing empathy and understanding of the user's needs and behaviors. It involves techniques such as user research, persona development, and iterative prototyping. Human-centered design has become increasingly popular in recent years as companies recognize the importance of creating user-centric products and services.

Gamification - This approach involves applying game design principles to non-game contexts, such as education, fitness, and productivity. By making activities more engaging and rewarding, gamification can motivate users to complete tasks and achieve goals. The concept of gamification has been around for decades, but it gained traction in the early 2010s as companies began experimenting with game-like features in their products and services.

UX design is not just about solving problems but also about creating opportunities. It's about identifying unmet needs and designing solutions that users didn't even know they needed. It's about creating experiences that inspire, delight, and exceed users' expectations. UX designers have the power to transform ordinary experiences into extraordinary ones by thinking innovatively and pushing the boundaries of what is possible.

Beyond the Surface: Uncovering the 'Why' in UX Design

In the world of UX design, we often get caught up in the "what" - the flashy features, the snazzy UI, the bells and whistles that make a product or service look oh-so-cool. But let me tell you a secret, my fellow UX aficionados: the real magic happens when you focus on the "why."

Now, I'm not talking about some existential crisis or philosophical pondering here. No, no, no. I'm talking about getting down to the nitty-gritty of understanding why users do what they do, and what really makes them tick. Because let's face it, users are complex creatures with motivations, desires, and emotions that drive their actions. And if you can crack that code, my friend, you've struck UX gold.

So, why is the "why" so important, you ask? Well, let me break it down for you in a way that even your grandma would understand.

Think of UX design like baking a cake. The "what" is the cake itself - the layers, the icing, the sprinkles on top. It's what everyone sees and oohs and ahhs over. But the "why" is the reason you're baking the cake in the first place - is it for a wedding, a kid's birthday, or a retirement party? Understanding the occasion behind the cake determines the flavor, the decorations, and the overall experience.

Sure, you can slap on some icing and sprinkles and call it a day. But without understanding the "why" behind the cake, you might end up with a cake that looks good but falls flat in taste and meaning.

So, how do you uncover the secret sauce of UX design? Well, it starts with understanding the "why" behind the user's actions. It's about getting to the heart of what really motivates users to use your product or service.

Let's take an example. Say you're designing a shopping app. The "what" might include features like a product catalog, a shopping cart, and a checkout process. But the "why" is what drives users to shop in the first place - the thrill of finding a great deal, the convenience of shopping from the comfort of their couch, the satisfaction of owning something new and shiny. Understanding these underlying motivations allows you to design an experience that taps into those emotions and creates a shopping experience that truly delights and engages users.

And it's not just about understanding the positive emotions. It's also about empathizing with the not-so-pleasant emotions that users may experience. Maybe they're frustrated with a clunky checkout process, or anxious about the security of their payment information. By addressing these pain points and alleviating those negative emotions, you can create an experience that builds trust and loyalty with your users.

But wait, there's more! Understanding the "why" also opens up a world of innovation. When you truly grasp what motivates users, you can come up with ingenious solutions that address their needs in unique and unexpected ways. It's like adding a sprinkle of creativity to your UX cake that takes it from basic to extraordinary.

So, my fellow UX warriors, let's not get caught up in the superficial "what" of UX design. Let's dig deeper, embrace the "why," and unlock the secret sauce that makes our designs truly magical. Because when it comes to UX, it's not just about making it pretty, it's about making it meaningful. So, go forth and sprinkle that secret sauce, and watch your UX designs soar to new heights of awesomeness!

Captivating User Experiences: The Power of Visual Storytelling in UX Design

Once upon a time in the world of User Experience (UX) design, there was a powerful tool known as Visual Storytelling. This magical technique used images, graphics, videos, and animations to create an engaging and memorable experience for users. It was based on the ancient principle that people process and remember information better when it is presented in a visual format, and it was wielded by skilled UX designers to create websites and apps that captivated the hearts and minds of their users.

To wield the power of visual storytelling in UX design, the first step for designers was to understand their audience and the story they wanted to tell. They delved deep into the world of user personas, user scenarios, and user research to uncover the desires, needs, and emotions of their users. Armed with this knowledge, they set out on an epic quest to create a user experience that would resonate with their audience.

The designers used a variety of visual elements in their storytelling arsenal. They wielded illustrations to build a narrative, guiding users through the story with visual cues that sparked their imagination. They used photos and graphics to enhance the copy, creating a visual feast for the eyes that drew users deeper into the experience. They harnessed the power of videos to tell a compelling story, evoking emotions and connecting with users on a deeper level. And they wielded animations like a sorcerer's spell, creating moments of delight and wonder that left users enchanted.

> **Design is an opportunity to continue telling the story, not just to sum everything up.**
>
> Tate Linden, the founder of Stokefire

But visual storytelling in UX design was not just about creating pretty pictures. It was about creating a sense of emotion, a connection with users that went beyond the surface. The designers understood that by triggering an emotional response, they could create an experience that users would remember long after they had closed the app or left the website. They used visuals to evoke specific emotions, whether it was joy, excitement, surprise, or even empathy. They crafted a journey that touched the hearts and minds of their users, leaving them with a lasting impression.

Visual storytelling in UX design was also about creating moments of delight and surprise. The designers knew that by adding unexpected visuals or animations, they could create a sense of wonder that would make the experience truly memorable. They sprinkled their designs with delightful surprises, like hidden Easter eggs, playful animations, or clever interactions that brought a smile to users' faces and made them want to explore further.

But the power of visual storytelling was not to be taken lightly. The designers knew that it had to be used with care and purpose. They considered the context and the goals of the experience, ensuring that every visual element served a specific purpose and contributed to the overall story they wanted to tell. They knew that visual storytelling was just one piece of the UX design puzzle, and it had to be combined with other techniques like user research, testing, and user-centered design to create a cohesive and satisfying user experience.

And so, the designers continued to wield the power of visual storytelling in their UX designs, creating websites and apps that were not just functional, but also captivating and memorable. Users across the land were drawn into the stories they told, becoming active participants in the experience. They laughed, they cried, they felt a connection, and they were delighted. And they continued to embark on new adventures, guided by the magic of visual storytelling in the world of UX design.

The End...or rather, the beginning of a new chapter in the world of visual storytelling in UX design, where creativity and empathy combine to create experiences that leave users spellbound and wanting more. So, go forth, fellow UX designers, and wield the power of visual storytelling to create user experiences that are truly magical!

Get Your UX Groove On: Mastering Terminology for Interview Success

If you're gearing up for a UX interview, you're in for an exciting ride! But before you buckle up and hit the road, it's essential to make sure you have the right lingo in your toolkit. Mastering UX terminology is like having the perfect set of wheels to navigate the design process with ease and confidence.

Why is terminology so important, you ask? Well, for starters, it's the language that UX professionals use to communicate effectively with each other. It's like having a secret code that unlocks a world of shared understanding and collaboration. Plus, using the right terminology during interviews shows that you know your stuff and can speak the language of the UX world fluently.

Sure, you might already be familiar with some basic UX terms like User Experience (UX) and User Interface (UI). But to really stand out during interviews, you need to take your UX lingo game to the next level. Let's dive into some awesome UX terms that will help you impress your interviewers and demonstrate your expertise.

- **A/B Testing:** This is a method of testing two or more versions of a design or feature with real users to determine which one performs better in terms of user engagement, conversion, or other predefined metrics. A/B testing helps you make data-driven decisions and optimize your designs based on actual user feedback.
- **Accessibility:** This refers to the design and development of products or services that can be used by people with disabilities. Ensuring accessibility in UX design means making sure that all users, regardless of their abilities, can access and use a product or service effectively.
- **Affordance:** This is the perceived functionality or potential use of an object or element based on its visual cues or design. For example, a button that looks like a button and is placed in a way that indicates it's

221

clickable has a strong affordance for users to interact with it.

· **Card Sorting:** This is a usability testing technique where users are asked to organize and categorize content or information into groups or categories that make sense to them. Card sorting helps to understand how users perceive and categorize information, which can inform the information architecture and organization of a product or service.

· **Cognitive Load:** This refers to the amount of mental effort or processing power required for users to understand and use a product or service. Minimizing cognitive load is important in UX design to ensure that users can easily process and understand the information presented to them without feeling overwhelmed or confused.

· **Dark Patterns:** Dark patterns are design techniques or elements that are intentionally used to manipulate or deceive users into taking actions that may not be in their best interest. Examples of dark patterns include misleading opt-in/opt-out checkboxes, hidden costs, or forced continuity. Ethical UX design should avoid using dark patterns and prioritize transparency and user empowerment.

· **Delighters:** These are unexpected, delightful interactions or features within a product or service that surprise and delight users. Delighters go beyond meeting basic user needs and create positive emotions, which can lead to increased user satisfaction, loyalty, and advocacy.

· **Design System:** A design system is a collection of guidelines, components, and patterns that establish a consistent visual and interactive language for a product or service. Design systems promote design consistency, efficiency, and scalability, and facilitate collaboration among designers and developers.

· **Emotional Design:** Emotional design is a design approach that considers the emotional response and experience of users when interacting with a product or service. Emotional design seeks to create positive emotional connections, delight, or evoke specific emotions through the design of interfaces, interactions, visuals, or other elements.

· **Error Messaging:** This is the design and presentation of messages that inform users about errors or issues that occur during their interactions with a product or service. Well-designed error messages can help users understand what went wrong, how to fix it, and what to do next, reducing frustration and improving the overall user experience.

· **Fitts' Law:** This is a mathematical formula that describes the relationship between the size of a target, the distance to the target, and the speed and accuracy of a user's movements. Understanding Fitts' Law can help you design interfaces that are easy to use and minimize errors by optimizing target size and spacing.

· **Flat Design:** Flat design is a minimalist design approach that focuses on simplicity, clean lines, and bold colors. It emphasizes the use of simple geometric shapes, such as squares, circles, and rectangles, without any added textures or gradients. Flat design often incorporates a minimalistic color palette, with bright and vibrant colors that create a visually appealing and modern aesthetic. This design approach is characterized by its straightforward and minimalistic visual style, which can help create a clean and uncluttered interface that is easy to understand and navigate. Flat design is often associated with a modern and sleek look, and it is commonly used in digital interfaces, such as websites and mobile applications.

· **Gamification:** This is the use of game-like elements, such as points, badges, or leaderboards, in non-game contexts to motivate and engage users. Understanding gamification can help you design products or services that are more enjoyable, motivating, and rewarding for users.

· **Gestalt Principles:** These are a set of psychological principles that describe how humans perceive and interpret visual elements. Understanding Gestalt principles, such as proximity, similarity, and closure, can help you create visually cohesive and appealing designs that users can quickly understand and interact with.

· **Google Material Design:** Google Material Design is a design language developed by Google that focuses on creating a consistent and intuitive user experience across different platforms and devices. It is based on the principles of flat design, but also incorporates depth, motion, and interactivity to create a more dynamic and engaging user interface.

Google Material Design uses a set of visual guidelines, such as the use of bold and colorful icons, typography, and responsive animations, to create a cohesive and visually appealing user experience. This design language is often used in Google's own products, such as Android applications and web interfaces, and has become widely adopted by other designers and developers as a standard for creating modern and visually appealing digital interfaces.

· **Haptic Feedback:** This is the use of tactile sensations, such as vibrations or touch, to provide feedback to users about their interactions with a product or service. Haptic feedback can enhance the overall user experience by adding an additional layer of sensory feedback, making interactions more engaging and intuitive.

· **Heatmap:** This is a visual representation of the areas of a design or interface that receive the most attention from users. Heatmaps are typically generated based on eye-tracking or mouse-tracking data and provide insights into how users interact with a design, helping to identify areas of interest or potential issues.

· **Information Architecture:** This refers to the way information is organized, labeled, and structured within a product or service. Good information architecture makes it easy for users to find what they're looking for, navigate through the content, and understand the relationships between different pieces of information.

· **Mental Models:** These are the cognitive frameworks or representations that users have in their minds about how a product or service should work based on their past experiences and knowledge. Understanding users' mental models can help you design interfaces and interactions that align with their expectations and reduce cognitive load.

· **Microcopy:** This refers to the small, concise, and meaningful snippets of text or copy within a design or interface that provide guidance, instructions, or feedback to users. Microcopy is an important aspect of UX writing and helps users understand how to interact with a design, recover from errors, and complete tasks successfully.

· **Microinteractions:** These are small, focused interactions or animations within a product or service that provide feedback, guidance, or delight to users. Examples of microinteractions include a "like" button changing color when clicked, a progress bar showing the status of a task, or a subtle animation indicating a successful action. Paying attention to microinteractions can greatly enhance the overall user experience and make your design stand out.

· **Progressive Disclosure:** This is a design technique where information is revealed to users gradually, based on their interactions or choices, instead of overwhelming them with too much information all at once. It's like peeling an onion, revealing one layer at a time, keeping users engaged and informed without overwhelming them.

· **Progressive Web Apps (PWAs):** PWAs are web applications that combine the features of web pages and native mobile apps to provide a seamless and app-like experience on web browsers. PWAs can be accessed and used offline, can be installed on home screens, and offer push notifications, among other features.

· **Service Design:** Service design is a holistic approach to designing the entire end-to-end experience of a service, including all the touchpoints and interactions between users and the service. Service design considers the entire service ecosystem, including people, processes, technologies, and physical environments, to create seamless and user-centric service experiences.

· **Serendipity:** This refers to the unexpected and pleasant discoveries or experiences that users may encounter while using a product or service.

· **Skeuomorphism:** Skeuomorphism is a design approach that uses visual cues or elements from the physical world to create familiar and intuitive digital interfaces. For example, using a virtual bookshelf with realistic book covers to represent a digital library. Skeuomorphism can create a sense of familiarity and ease of use for users.

· **Storyboarding:** Storyboarding is a visual storytelling technique used in UX design to create a sequence of images or sketches that represent the user experience or interaction flow. Storyboards can help designers communicate design ideas, explore different design solutions, and get feedback from stakeholders or users.

· **Visual Hierarchy:** This refers to the arrangement and presentation of visual elements in a design to guide users' attention and prioritize information. Understanding visual hierarchy helps you create designs that are visually appealing, easy to scan, and convey information in a clear and organized manner.

· **White Space:** Also known as negative space, white space is the empty space between design elements, such as text, images, and buttons. White space is important in UX design as it helps to create visual breathing room, improves readability, and guides users' focus on key elements, making the design more visually appealing and user-friendly.

Using the correct terminology in UX interviews not only demonstrates your expertise but also helps you communicate effectively with other UX professionals. Familiarizing yourself with these UX terms and incorporating them into your design process can elevate your UX game and impress your interviewers. So, get your UX groove on and rock your next UX interview with confidence!

Mastering the Art of Presenting and Demonstrating Your UX Work

Effective communication is a critical aspect of a UX designer's job when presenting and demonstrating their work. Whether it is showcasing designs to stakeholders, conducting usability testing sessions, or presenting a portfolio in an interview, the ability to communicate effectively can make all the difference. Here are three examples of how you can excel in presenting and demonstrating your UX work:

Know Your Audience

Before you start presenting or demonstrating your work, it's essential to understand your audience. Who are you presenting to? What are their roles and responsibilities? What are their priorities and interests? Tailor your communication style and content accordingly to resonate with your audience. For example, if you're presenting to executives, focus on the business impact and ROI of your UX work. If you're presenting to developers, highlight the technical aspects and implementation details. Knowing your audience and customizing your communication approach can help you connect with them on a more meaningful level.

Be Clear and Concise

When presenting or demonstrating your UX work, it's crucial to be clear and concise in your communication. Avoid using jargon or technical terms that your audience may not be familiar with. Instead, use simple and straightforward language to convey your ideas. Clearly articulate the problem you were trying to solve, your design approach, and the outcomes or results of your work. Use visuals, such as wireframes, prototypes, or screenshots, to support your explanations and make your work more tangible to your audience. Being clear and concise in your communication helps to ensure that your message is easily understood and remembered.

Show, Don't Just Tell

Demonstrating your work effectively is a crucial aspect of being a UX designer. You have the advantage of using visual tools to showcase your designs, which can be much more effective than just talking about them.

To show your designs in action, you can use live demos, interactive prototypes, or screen recordings. This hands-on approach allows your audience to experience the user journey and interact with your designs, making it more engaging and memorable. By demonstrating how your

UX work functions and how it addresses user needs, you can effectively communicate the value of your designs.

Furthermore, using real-world examples or case studies can help illustrate the impact of your UX work on actual users or business goals. By showing your work in action, you can make a compelling case for your design decisions and their value.

Presenting and demonstrating your UX work requires effective communication skills. By knowing your audience, being clear and concise, and using visual tools to show your ideas you can excel in presenting and demonstrating your UX work. With these tips, you can confidently showcase your UX work and make a lasting impression on your stakeholders, users, and potential employers.

* * *

Chapter 15: Career in UX

Are you fascinated by the seamless experiences of your favorite apps or websites? Do you find yourself critically evaluating the usability and user-friendliness of digital products? Are you passionate about creating products that solve real-world problems and improve people's lives? If so, then a career in User Experience (UX) design might just be the perfect fit for you!

In this chapter, we will provide insights for those considering a career in this field. Whether you are a recent graduate, a career changer, or someone looking to add new skills to your repertoire, this chapter will give you a glimpse into the world of UX design and help you embark on this thrilling journey.

Why Choose a Career in UX Design?

The field of UX design offers a unique blend of creativity, psychology, research, and technology, making it a highly rewarding and fulfilling career choice. Here are some compelling reasons why you might consider pursuing a career in UX design:

- **Impactful Work:** As a UX designer, you have the opportunity to create products that positively impact people's lives. You get to design experiences that are not only aesthetically pleasing but also user-friendly, accessible, and meaningful. Your work can improve how people interact with technology, solve real-world problems, and enhance their overall experience.
- **Growing Demand:** The demand for UX designers is on the rise across various industries, including technology, finance, healthcare, e-commerce, and more. Companies are recognizing the value of user-centered design and the impact it can have on their bottom line. This presents ample career opportunities and growth prospects for UX designers in the job market.
- **Diverse Skill Set:** UX design is a multidisciplinary field that requires a diverse skill set. From conducting user research and creating wireframes to designing visual interfaces and testing usability, UX designers wear many hats. This provides a dynamic and ever-evolving work environment that keeps you challenged and engaged.
- **Collaboration and Innovation:** UX design is a collaborative field that involves working closely with cross-functional teams, including product managers, developers, marketers, and stakeholders. This collaborative approach fosters innovation, creativity, and a culture of continuous learning and improvement.
- **Flexibility and Versatility:** UX design offers flexibility in terms of work settings and opportunities for remote work. Additionally, the skills

acquired in UX design are versatile and can be applied to various domains, making it a valuable asset for career growth and exploration.

Is UX Design Right for You?

While a career in UX design can be rewarding, it is important to evaluate whether it is the right fit for you. UX design requires a unique blend of skills, traits, and mindset. Here are some key qualities that can indicate if UX design might be the right career path for you:

Empathy: UX design is all about understanding and empathizing with users. You need to be able to put yourself in the shoes of the users, understand their needs, motivations, and pain points, and design solutions that cater to their requirements.

Creativity: UX design requires creative problem-solving skills to come up with innovative and user-friendly solutions. You need to be able to think critically, approach problems from different angles, and come up with creative solutions that are both functional and visually appealing.

Analytical Thinking: UX design involves analyzing data and making data-driven decisions. You need to be able to analyze user research findings, feedback, and performance metrics to inform your design decisions and continuously improve the user experience.

Strong Communication Skills: UX design is a collaborative field that requires effective communication with team members, stakeholders, and users. You need to be able to articulate your design ideas, justify your design decisions, and effectively communicate your design solutions to different audiences.

Attention to Detail: UX design involves meticulous attention to detail to ensure that every interaction, visual element, and functionality is designed with precision. Small design details can have a big impact on the overall user experience, and it's essential to have an eye for detail to ensure a seamless and delightful user experience.

Attention to details what makes the final piece superior.

Ahmed AlAnsari, the founder and creative director of AlAnsari Studios

Flexibility and Adaptability: UX design is an ever-evolving field with changing technologies, design trends, and user expectations. You need to be adaptable and open to learning new tools, techniques, and methodologies. Flexibility in adjusting your design approach based on feedback and changing requirements is crucial in UX design.

Passion for User-Centered Design: UX design is all about designing with the user in mind. You need to have a genuine passion for understanding users, their behaviors, and their needs. Putting the user at the center of your design process and advocating for their needs is essential in UX design.

Resilience and Problem-Solving Skills: UX design can come with challenges, such as tight deadlines, conflicting feedback, and technical constraints. You need to have the resilience to overcome these challenges and the problem-solving skills to find creative solutions to complex design problems.

Continuous Learning Mindset: UX design is a field that is constantly evolving, and it's crucial to have a continuous learning mindset. Staying updated with the latest design trends, technologies, and methodologies and constantly improving your skills through learning and professional development is essential in UX design.

A career in UX design can be an exciting and fulfilling journey for those who are passionate about creating user-centric digital experiences. It offers a unique blend of creativity, empathy, research, and technology, with ample opportunities for growth and impact. However, it's essential to evaluate if UX design is the right fit for you based on your skills, traits, and mindset. If you have a passion for understanding users, solving problems creatively, and constantly improving the user experience, then UX design might just be the perfect career path for you! So, strap on your creativity hat, sharpen your analytical skills, and get ready to embark on the exciting journey of UX design.

Best Professions for UX Design Career Changers

While UX design is a broad field with many career opportunities, certain professions tend to be a good fit for UX career beginners due to the transferability of skills. Here are some examples:

Graphic Designers: With their expertise in visual design, layout, and typography, graphic designers have a strong foundation for transitioning into UX design. They can leverage their skills in creating aesthetically pleasing and user-friendly interfaces, as well as their understanding of branding and visual storytelling.

Web Developers: Web developers, especially those with front-end development experience, have a solid understanding of coding principles and web technologies. They can leverage their coding skills to create interactive and responsive user interfaces, as well as their understanding of user behavior and usability.

Marketers/Communications Professionals: Professionals with a background in marketing or communications have a deep understanding of user behavior, user research, and messaging. They can apply their skills in crafting compelling user experiences, understanding target audiences, and conducting market research to inform their UX designs.

Psychologists/Human Factors Specialists: Professionals with a background in psychology or human factors can leverage their understanding of human behavior, cognition, and ergonomics to inform their UX designs. They are skilled in conducting user research, analyzing data, and creating user-centered experiences.

Project Managers: Project managers are skilled in planning, organizing, and coordinating complex projects. They can leverage their project management expertise to ensure UX projects are delivered on time and within budget, and to effectively communicate with cross-functional teams, stakeholders, and clients.

Customer Service Representatives: Professionals with experience in customer service have a deep understanding of user needs and are skilled in effectively communicating with users to address their concerns, provide solutions, and ensure their satisfaction. Their experience in handling customer inquiries, resolving issues, and maintaining a positive customer experience gives them valuable insights into user behaviors, preferences, and pain points. This understanding of user needs can be invaluable in UX design, as it helps designers create intuitive, user-friendly interfaces, anticipate potential user issues, and design solutions that meet user expectations. Customer service representatives bring a unique perspective to UX design, with their ability to empathize with users and provide exceptional service, making them a valuable asset to any UX design team.

Architects/Industrial Designers: Architects and industrial designers are trained in understanding human behavior, spatial design, and ergonomics. They can apply their skills in creating intuitive and user-friendly physical spaces to digital experiences. Their understanding of user flow, information hierarchy, and aesthetics can be invaluable in crafting seamless and visually appealing user experiences.

Teachers/Instructional Designers: Teachers and instructional designers have a strong understanding of pedagogy, learning theories, and instructional design principles. They can leverage their skills in creating effective and engaging learning experiences to design user-centric digital products. Their ability to analyze user needs, create user personas, and design instructional content can inform their UX designs and create meaningful interactions.

Anthropologists/Sociologists: Professionals with a background in anthropology or sociology have a deep understanding of human behavior, cultural norms, and social dynamics. They can leverage their skills in conducting ethnographic research, analyzing data, and understanding user motivations to inform their UX designs. Their ability to empathize with diverse user groups and design inclusive experiences can create products that cater to the needs of a wide range of users.

Writers/Content Creators: Writers and content creators are skilled in crafting compelling narratives, storytelling, and content strategy. They can leverage their skills in creating engaging and user-centric content for digital products, such as websites, apps, or interactive experiences. Their ability to understand user needs, create user-friendly copy, and ensure a consistent tone and voice can greatly enhance the overall user experience.

Data Analysts/Researchers: Data analysts and researchers have expertise in collecting, analyzing, and interpreting data. They can apply their skills in conducting user research, analyzing user data, and making data-driven decisions to inform their UX designs. Their ability to identify patterns, trends, and insights from data can help create data-informed and user-centered designs.

Gamers/Design Thinkers: Gamers and design thinkers have a unique perspective on user experience as they understand the intricacies of interaction, engagement, and feedback loops. They can apply their skills in understanding player behavior, game mechanics, and game design principles to create engaging and immersive user experiences in digital products. Their ability to think critically, solve problems, and iterate on designs can be valuable in creating user-centric products.

UX design is a field that welcomes career beginners from diverse backgrounds. While some may have formal UX education or experience, others bring with them a valuable set of transferable skills from their previous careers. The key is to leverage these skills, adapt and apply them to the unique challenges of UX design. So, whether you're a fresh-faced graduate, a bootcamp bounty hunter, or a career chameleon, remember that your previous career skills can be an asset in your UX design journey. Embrace your unique background, keep learning, and let your skills shine in the world of UX design!

Crafting Your Perfect First Portfolio

As a UX designer with limited work experience, your portfolio plays a crucial role in showcasing your skills, creativity, and potential to potential employers. A well-designed and compelling portfolio can make a lasting impression and increase your chances of landing your first UX job. Here are some actionable tips to help you create a perfect first portfolio:

Choose the Right Platform

There are several online platforms that allow you to create a free portfolio website easily. Some popular options include:

- Behance (www.behance.net)
- Dribbble (www.dribbble.com)
- WordPress (www.wordpress.com)
- Wix (www.wix.com)
- Squarespace (www.squarespace.com)

These platforms provide user-friendly templates and customization options that allow you to create a professional-looking portfolio without any coding skills. Choose a platform that aligns with your design style and provides the features you need to showcase your work effectively.

Note: Please ensure to review the terms and conditions, privacy policy, and any associated fees of these platforms before creating your portfolio to make an informed decision.

Keep It Simple and User-Friendly

When it comes to portfolio design, less is often more. Avoid cluttering your portfolio with too much information or too many design elements. Keep the design clean, simple, and easy to navigate. Use a consistent color scheme, typography, and layout that aligns with your personal brand and the UX design principles you've learned.

Make sure your portfolio is mobile-friendly, as potential employers may view it on different devices. Test your portfolio on different screen sizes to ensure a seamless user experience across all devices.

Showcase Your Best Work

As a beginner, it's better to focus on quality over quantity. Include only your best and most relevant projects in your portfolio. Aim for 3-5 projects that demonstrate a diverse range of skills, such as user research, interaction design, visual design, and prototyping.

Provide a brief description of each project, including the problem you were trying to solve, your design process, and the outcomes or results. Showcase the final deliverables, such as wireframes, prototypes, and visual designs, along with any relevant research findings or user feedback.

Demonstrate Your Design Process

In addition to showcasing the final outcomes, it's important to highlight your design process in your portfolio. Explain how you approached each project, the research methods you used, the design decisions you made, and the tools or software you employed. Including your design process shows your ability to think critically, problem-solve, and follow a structured approach to UX design.

Consider including case studies for each project that provide a deeper insight into your design process. Use visuals, such as diagrams, sketches, and screenshots, to illustrate your design thinking and decision-making.

Highlight Your Skills and Expertise

As a UX designer with limited work experience, it's important to highlight your skills and expertise in your portfolio. Showcase your proficiency in relevant tools and software, such as Sketch, Figma, Adobe XD, or InVision. Mention any coding skills or knowledge of front-end technologies, if applicable.

Include any relevant certifications, courses, or workshops you have completed to showcase your commitment to continuous learning and professional development. Highlight any industry-specific knowledge or domain expertise you possess, such as healthcare, finance, or e-commerce, if relevant to the jobs you are applying for.

Include a Call-to-Action

Don't forget to include a clear call-to-action in your portfolio, such as a "Contact Me" or "Hire Me" button. Make it easy for potential employers to reach out to you by providing your email address, LinkedIn profile, or other relevant contact information. Show your eagerness and availability for new opportunities.

Seek Feedback and Iterate

Before launching your portfolio, seek feedback from mentors, peers, or industry professionals. Ask for their input on the design, content, and overall presentation of your portfolio. Take their feedback into consideration and make necessary improvements to ensure that your portfolio is polished and reflects your best work.

Once your portfolio is live, continue to iterate and update it as you gain more experience and complete new projects. Keep it fresh and relevant by regularly updating your projects, skills, and certifications.

Be Mindful of Intellectual Property and NDAs

As a UX designer, you may have worked on projects that are protected by non-disclosure agreements (NDAs) or other intellectual property (IP) rights. Be mindful of these restrictions when creating your portfolio. Avoid sharing any confidential or proprietary information that could violate NDAs or IP rights. If you are unsure about what can be included in your portfolio, seek permission from the relevant parties before showcasing any work.

Be Authentic and Tell Your Story

Finally, be authentic and tell your unique story in your portfolio. Share your passion for UX design, your motivation for pursuing a career in this field, and your personal design philosophy. Be genuine in your communication and showcase your personality through your portfolio. Employers value authenticity and want to see the real you shine through.

Landing Your First UX Job Without Prior Work Experience

Congratulations on completing your UX design portfolio! It's a significant achievement that showcases your skills and creativity as a UX designer. However, as a recent graduate from school or a bootcamp, you might find that many job postings require 2-3 years of work experience, which can feel daunting when you're just starting your career. But don't worry, there are still plenty of opportunities to land your first UX job and kickstart your career. In this chapter, we will explore strategies and tips on how to find your first UX job without prior work experience.

Leverage Your Education and Bootcamp Experience

Although you may not have professional work experience, your education and bootcamp training are valuable assets. Highlight your coursework, projects, and any relevant certifications in your resume and cover letter. Describe the UX design methodologies, tools, and techniques you learned, and how you applied them to real-world projects. Emphasize any collaboration or team projects, as they demonstrate your ability to work effectively in a team setting.

Network and Connect with the UX Community

Networking can be a powerful way to discover job opportunities and make connections in the UX industry. Attend UX meetups, industry events, and conferences to meet other UX professionals and potential employers. Join online communities, such as UX design forums, LinkedIn groups, or UX design Slack channels, to connect with other professionals and learn about job openings. Don't be afraid to reach out to UX designers or mentors for advice or informational interviews. Building a strong professional network can lead to job referrals or recommendations, even if you don't have prior work experience.

Look for Internship or Entry-Level Opportunities

Many companies offer internships or entry-level positions specifically for recent graduates or candidates with minimal work experience. Look for job postings that explicitly state they are open to hiring candidates with little or no experience. These opportunities can provide you with valuable on-the-job experience, mentorship, and a chance to build your professional network. Don't be discouraged if the job title or salary is not what you expected at first. Remember, gaining experience and building your portfolio should be your priority at this stage of your career.

Be Proactive and Create Your Own Opportunities

Don't wait for job postings to come to you. Be proactive and create your own opportunities. Reach out to companies or startups you are interested in and inquire about potential job openings or internships. Offer to do a small project or volunteer your services to gain practical experience and demonstrate your skills. Consider freelance or contract work, which can be a stepping stone to a full-time position. Build your online presence through a personal website, blog, or social media to showcase your skills and attract potential employers.

Keep Learning and Upskilling

The field of UX design is constantly evolving, and it's important to stay updated with the latest trends, tools, and techniques. Continuously improve your skills and knowledge through online courses, workshops, or certifications. Develop expertise in a specific area of UX, such as interaction design, information architecture, or usability testing, to make yourself stand out. Show your willingness to learn and adapt to changes in the industry, as this demonstrates your dedication to professional growth and development. Stay curious, read UX blogs, follow industry leaders on social media, and engage in discussions about UX design topics. The more knowledgeable and skilled you are, the more attractive you will be to potential employers.

Tailor Your Application and Interview Approach

When applying for a UX job, make sure to customize your resume and cover letter for each job application. Highlight relevant skills, experiences, and projects that align with the specific job requirements. Show how your skills and expertise can contribute to the company's goals and address their pain points. During interviews, be prepared to discuss your portfolio and projects in detail, and explain your design process, decision-making, and outcomes. Be honest about your lack of work experience but showcase your eagerness to learn and contribute to the team. Demonstrate your problem-solving skills, critical thinking, and ability to work well in a team environment.

Showcase Your Soft Skills

Even though you may not have much work experience, you likely have developed valuable soft skills through your education and bootcamp training. Soft skills, such as communication, collaboration, time management, and adaptability, are highly sought after in the UX industry. Highlight these skills in your resume, cover letter, and interviews, and provide examples of how you have demonstrated them in your projects or group work. Employers value candidates who can work well with others, communicate effectively, and be adaptable in a fast-paced, collaborative UX environment.

Be Persistent and Stay Positive

Landing your first UX job may take time and effort, but it's important to stay persistent and positive. Don't get discouraged by rejections or lack of response from job applications. Keep applying, networking, and refining your skills and portfolio. Seek feedback from mentors or industry professionals to improve your chances of success. Stay positive and confident in your abilities, as employers are not only looking for experience but also potential and attitude. Your passion for UX design and determination to succeed can make a lasting impression on potential employers.

Keep an Open Mind and Embrace Opportunities

When starting your career, it's important to keep an open mind and be willing to embrace opportunities that may not be exactly what you initially envisioned. Consider different types of UX roles, such as freelance, contract, or remote work, to gain experience and build your portfolio. Be open to working with different industries or niches, as UX design is applicable to various fields. Don't be afraid to step out of your comfort zone and take on new challenges, as they can lead to valuable experiences and opportunities for growth.

Finding your first UX job without prior work experience can be challenging, but it's not impossible. By leveraging your education and bootcamp experience, building a strong portfolio, networking, being proactive, continuously learning and improving your skills, showcasing your soft skills, staying persistent and positive, and keeping an open mind, you can increase your chances of landing your first UX job. Remember that gaining experience, building your portfolio, and establishing your professional network are key priorities at this stage of your career. Stay committed to your goals, be patient, and keep refining your skills and approach. With determination, perseverance, and the right strategies, you can successfully launch your UX career and take the first steps towards a fulfilling and rewarding professional journey. Good luck!

The Key Traits for Success in UX Design and Insights from a Hiring Manager

The hiring manager has developed a belief that the crucial factors for successful recruitment and hiring in the UX design industry are **character**, **attitude**, and **reliability**. These traits are highly valuable and can potentially surpass other skills that can be acquired through on-the-job training. The following section will delve into the significance of these qualities for novice designers and provide insights from the perspective of a hiring manager.

Character: The Foundation of a Great Designer

Character refers to the inherent qualities and values that an individual possesses. In UX design, having good character is essential as it influences how a designer approaches their work and interacts with team members and clients. A designer with strong character traits, such as integrity, professionalism, and a strong work ethic, is more likely to be trustworthy, dependable, and accountable for their actions. These qualities are essential in the fast-paced and collaborative environment of UX design, where designers need to work closely with team members, communicate effectively, and meet deadlines.

Attitude: The Driving Force for Success

Attitude plays a significant role in the success of a UX designer. A positive attitude towards work, challenges, and feedback can greatly impact a designer's ability to learn, adapt, and grow. A designer with a positive attitude is open to new ideas, willing to take risks, and eager to learn from mistakes. They approach challenges with a problem-solving mindset, and they are not afraid to seek help or collaborate with others. A positive attitude also reflects in a designer's ability to communicate effectively and build positive relationships with team members, clients, and stakeholders.

Reliability: The Pillar of Trust

Reliability is a critical trait that distinguishes a good designer from a great one. A reliable designer is someone who can be counted on to deliver high-quality work consistently and meet deadlines. They are dependable, responsible, and committed to their work. They take ownership of their tasks and follow through on their commitments. Reliability is crucial in UX design, where projects often have tight deadlines and require timely deliverables. A reliable designer builds trust with their team and clients, which is essential for a successful working relationship.

Recommended Reading for UX Designers

As experienced UX leaders, we acknowledge that we stand on the shoulders of giants - the UX experts who have paved the way with their wisdom, experience, and insights. These authors have provided us with the necessary resources and knowledge to navigate the world of UX design, and we are grateful for their contributions to the field.

Here are some recommended readings that have inspired and informed the content of this book, and are essential for all UX designers looking to further their knowledge and expertise:

- "The Design of Everyday Things" by Don Norman - This classic book introduces the principles of user-centered design, emphasizing the importance of understanding users and designing products that meet their needs.
- "The Inmates Are Running the Asylum" by Alan Cooper - A thought-provoking book that challenges traditional software development practices and advocates for a user-centric approach to design and development.
- "Don't Make Me Think" by Steve Krug - This practical guide to usability and web design emphasizes the importance of creating intuitive and easy-to-use interfaces that minimize cognitive load for users.
- "Seductive Interaction Design" by Stephen Anderson - This book explores how to create engaging and compelling user experiences through the use of visual design, storytelling, and emotional appeal.
- "The Elements of User Experience" by Jesse James Garrett - This comprehensive book outlines the different components of user experience design, from strategy and scope to structure and surface, providing a holistic understanding of UX.
- "Universal Principles of Design" by William Lidwell, Kritina Holden, and Jill Butler - This reference book covers 125 principles of design, including those related to usability, information architecture, and visual design, providing practical guidelines for creating effective user experiences.
- "Information Architecture: For the Web and Beyond" by Louis Rosenfeld and Peter Morville - This guide provides insights into creating effective information architectures for digital products, including websites and apps, which are essential for organizing and presenting content in a user-friendly way.
- "Interviewing Users: How to Uncover Compelling Insights" by Steve Portigal - This book offers practical guidance on conducting user interviews to uncover deep insights about user needs, behaviors, and motivations, which can inform the design process.
- "Measuring the User Experience" by Thomas Tullis and William Albert - This book covers various methods for measuring the usability and

effectiveness of user experiences, including surveys, usability testing, and analytics, which are crucial for evaluating the success of UX design efforts.

• "About Face: The Essentials of Interaction Design" by Alan Cooper, Robert Reimann, and David Cronin - This comprehensive guide covers interaction design principles and best practices for creating user-friendly interfaces, providing practical insights on how to design interfaces that are intuitive and easy to use.

The authors of the recommended readings have made significant contributions to the field of UX design, providing valuable insights and perspectives on the challenges and opportunities in this domain. Exploring these readings can help aspiring UX designers learn from the vast wealth of knowledge and experience shared by experts in the field.

It is important to critically evaluate and apply these principles and practices in the context of specific projects and users. Remember that theory is not always the same as real practical experience, so strive to balance theory with practical application. As a UX designer, one should never stop learning and growing in their craft.

* * *

Conclusion

Throughout this exciting journey exploring the world of UX, we have encountered various obstacles and gained valuable insights into the art of designing for users. As we come to the end of this journey, let's take a moment to reflect on the challenges we faced and the lessons we learned along the way. Despite the complexities and contradictions that exist in the realm of UX, there is still beauty to be found in the process of creating user-centric designs.

UX is like a puzzle with constantly shifting pieces. Just when you think you've figured out the perfect wireframe or user flow, a stakeholder throws a curveball with their preference for a different color or font size. But hey, that's just part of the UX adventure! It's a chance to practice flexibility, adaptability, and creative problem-solving. It's an opportunity to find the delicate balance between user-centric design and stakeholder expectations, and create a harmonious blend that delivers a meaningful experience to users while achieving business goals.

As a UX designer, you may have encountered the gap between UX theory and UX reality. The ideal process you learned in school may not always align with the practicalities of working in the field. You've learned that sometimes compromises need to be made, timelines need to be adjusted, and expectations need to be managed. But fear not, for this is where your UX expertise shines! You know how to navigate through the complexities of real-world projects, adapt your process to fit different contexts, and make data-driven decisions that drive meaningful outcomes.

And let's not forget the importance of user feedback! It's the lifeblood of UX design, helping you understand what's working, what's not, and how to iterate and improve. It's a chance to gather insights from the real users who are at the heart of your design decisions. You've learned that feedback is not criticism, but an invaluable opportunity for growth and refinement. It's a chance to show empathy, listen deeply, and collaborate with users to create a product that truly meets their needs.

So, dear UX designers, as you continue your UX journey, remember that UX is not just about theory, but also about the reality of the ever-changing landscape of user needs, stakeholder expectations, and real-world constraints. Embrace the chaos with curiosity, resilience, and a growth mindset. Keep learning, experimenting, and refining your UX skills. Stay true to the core principles of UX, while adapting your process to fit the unique challenges of each project. And never forget the power of user feedback in shaping a user-centric product.

As you move forward in your UX career, may you continue to thrive in the wild world of UX, finding joy in the challenges, celebrating the wins, and making a meaningful impact on the lives of users. You are the next generation of UX designers, shaping the future of user experiences with your creativity, passion, and expertise. Keep practicing UX, and remember, the sky's the limit! Here's to a future filled with endless possibilities and remarkable UX adventures. Onward and upward!

* * *

www.ingramcontent.com/pod-product-compliance
Lightning Source LLC
LaVergne TN
LVHW051732050326
832903LV00023B/895